Adventures in the Father's Joy!

Mission Stories for the New Evangelization

Fr. Lawrence Edward Tucker, SOLT

ENROUTE
Books and Media

En Route Books and Media, LLC
5705 Rhodes Avenue
St. Louis, MO 63109

Cover credit: TJ Burdick

Library of Congress Control Number: 2017947535

ISBN-10:0-9991143-4-4
ISBN-13:978-0-9991143-4-6

DEDICATION

To the poor… who are so often forgotten.

"This is why I want a Church which is poor and for the poor. They have much to teach us. Not only do they share in the *sensus fidei*, but in their difficulties they know the suffering Christ. We need to let ourselves be evangelized by them. The new evangelization is an invitation to acknowledge the saving power at work in their lives and to put them at the center of the Church's pilgrim way. We are called to find Christ in them, to lend our voice to their causes, but also to be their friends, to listen to them, to speak for them and to embrace the mysterious wisdom which God wishes to share with us through them."

Pope Francis

(*Evangelii Gaudium*, 198)

CONTENTS

ACKNOWLEDGEMENTS

Over the years, the Lord has provided me with many friends who refused to forget the poor. These friends, through their generous support, have helped me bring the Good News to the poor.

It would be impossible to list them all... and most would prefer to remain anonymous. They know who they are... and Jesus, the Good Shepherd, knows who they are (*"I know my sheep."* John 10: 14).

They come from all walks of life, but have one thing in common; the desire to help their heavenly Father serve his beloved children who have been excluded and forgotten.

"No one can say that they cannot be close to the poor because their own lifestyle demands more attention to other areas."

POPE FRANCIS

(*Evangelii Gaudium*, 201)

TESTIMONIALS

"If you're like me, you know how a good missionary brings to life the heart, mind, and soul of the Gospel. Well... we have such a good missionary in Father Larry Tucker. From his daily experiences as a missionary, he has woven stories that help us experience the Greatest Story ever told... the life and love of Jesus Christ for his people! Allow Father Tucker to take you along with him to encounter Jesus and his Church." - *Msgr. Richard M. Figliozzi, Office of New Evangelization (former Director), Diocese of Rockville Centre, NY.*

"I love these inspiring mission adventure stories! They fill me with a great desire to serve and to participate in the New Evangelization. In an age saddened by materialism and indifference, college and university students will find hope in these stories because they show that, contrary to popular opinion, there is more joy in giving than in receiving!" - *Michaela Henry, 21, Student- Molloy College, Long Island, NY*

"It is one thing to read, hear, and speak God's Word. It is quite another to have a missionary such as Father Larry live Christ's Word every moment of every day... a missionary that inspires and motivates us to weave the Spirit into our lives and let the Father's joy flourish so abundantly that we want to share it with everyone!" - *Ruben R. Gonzalez, Knight of The Equestrian Order of The Holy Sepulchre, Yale University Alumnus, and General Partner- Trium, Ltd.*

"Father Larry Tucker's accounts of his missionary journeys are not only very descriptive and inspiring... they are also hilarious at times! I shared one of his experiences described in the book; the discovery of the image of Our Lady of Guadalupe in Robstown, TX. Reading his account of that event brought back many happy memories! You will be entertained by these adventurous stories… and motivated by them to enter into the joy of the New Evangelization!" - *Fr. Robert Shaldone, SOLT: National Spiritual Director of The Lay Missionaries of Charity (St. Mother Teresa's congregation).*

FOREWORD BY RONDA CHERVIN

With all the Catholics who have become discouraged by news of priests and sisters giving up on these vocations and news of others giving into terrible temptations, what could be more hopeful than memoirs of a joyful, faithful priest!

I met Fr. Larry Tucker some 20 years ago in Corpus Christi, Texas, where I was teaching at a little college run by the Society of Our Lady of the Most Holy Trinity, otherwise known as SOLT.

I was refreshed by his enthusiastic approach to, well, everything!

Whereas some of us, even if we are 24/7 Catholics, give into the vice of grinding and gnashing our teeth whenever we are frustrated in our goals, Fr. Larry manages to laugh!

His accounts of his adventures as a young priest will have you laughing, too. But they will also give you reasons to pray for greater strength to "fight the good fight."

The book would be wonderful to give to any young or older men you think might be called to ministry as priests in a diocese or to membership in religious communities.

Enjoy!

Ronda Chervin, Ph.D. is a retired professor emeritus of philosophy at Holy Apostles College and Seminary, author of numerous Catholic books and a presenter on Catholic TV and radio.

PREFACE

Like so many of the priests, sisters and laity in the Society of Our Lady of the Most Holy Trinity (SOLT), Fr. Larry Tucker discovered the "pearl of great price" while serving in the SOLT missions of Central America.

It is amazing how many of our members have either discovered their vocations while serving in mission or experienced some of the greatest years of their religious life while there. While the demands are high, the service to those in need and the experience of God's Providence amidst great challenges leads one to truly marvel at the goodness and power of God, and to experience tremendous peace, joy and fulfillment.

In *Adventures in the Father's Joy!*, Fr. Larry recounts his own experiences while serving in SOLT missions in Central America. His book is his personal testimony and affirmation of everything Pope Francis speaks about in *Evangelii Gaudium* ("The Joy of the Gospel") – there is great joy to be found in following Christ and living the Gospel. Hopefully, Fr. Larry's experiences will inspire others to discover that same joy!

- Fr. Peter Marsalek, SOLT, STD, General Priest Servant

Fr. Lawrence Edward Tucker, SOLT

INTRODUCTION

"Who are these beautiful people smiling at me and waving hello?"… I wondered as I began to regain consciousness. Every window on the beat-up, 18-year-old Toyota was filled with numerous grinning faces. I was curled up on the back seat, having fallen into a deep sleep following a grueling 4-day overland journey from Brownsville, TX, to Benque Viejo, Belize. So profound was my sleep I didn't even realize we had arrived at the mission and that Fr. John and Deacon Victor had already exited the vehicle.

Like Lazarus, who was raised by the voice of Jesus, I was roused from my slumber by the sweet voices of the gentle Mayan people who had gathered to welcome the new missionary… "Wake up, Larry! Welcome, Larry!" When I opened my eyes and saw those happy, youthful faces peering in at me my heart was filled with an infused joy which, in retrospect, was a most fitting inauguration for the wonder that is missionary life.

As I lay there transfixed, allowing myself time to drink in the unspeakable beauty of the scene before me, I noticed in the background the bell-tower of the ancient limestone church and, alongside it, an enormous royal palm tree. Clearly, I was no longer in New York City! I couldn't help but think, "How did this happen? How does someone from Manhattan wake up one day in a completely new world of heart-stopping beauty and endless surprises?"

The answer is really quite simple; one need only hear God's call (remembering that every baptized person is called!) and respond from the heart… "Here I am Lord, send me!" (Isaiah 6: 8)… and the

1

journey begins! A very wise missionary priest once told me that he believed the greatest blessing a person could receive was to be sent by God on a mission to serve the poor. I have personally experienced the truth of those words and, in the pages that follow, will attempt to share the joy of missionary life.

Since the completion of the second Vatican Council, the Church has been moving ever more deeply into its essential missionary identity. With the election of Pope Francis and the publication of his Apostolic Exhortation, *The Joy of the Gospel* (Evangelii Gaudium= EG), that movement of the Church into its core identity has been brought into such perfect focus that many people in the Church have been caught off guard. Suddenly… we are all missionaries! As Pope Francis likes to say… *"Surprise!"*

In my travels as a missionary priest, I have noticed that most people have a very limited and sometimes even distorted understanding of missionary life. There is a tendency to see missionary work in a negative, worldly way; as though the missionary was not called and sent by God but was acting alone with nothing other than limited human strength combined with questionable motives. Missionary work, therefore, is seen as being much too demanding for the average person and is meant only for the most robust and zealous among us.

"Surprise!" Nothing could be further from the truth! Every person baptized into the dynamic life of the Triune God is called to serve… no one is excluded. Missionary life is pure joy… it's like walking on water! God does the "heavy lifting"… and the missionary holds on for the ride of a lifetime! In the stories that follow, I hope to present the gift of missionary life, not as the world sees it… but as God sees it. Enjoy the ride!

"In virtue of their baptism, all the members of the people of God have become missionary disciples (cf. Mt 28: 19)…The new evangelization calls for

personal involvement on the part of each of the baptized." (EG, 120)

(The characters in the following stories are real... although in certain instances their names are fictitious. The stories are based on a composite of providential events that took place in the course of missionary activity. While it is impossible to perfectly recall dialogue, along with the less significant details of incidents that unfolded many years ago, the essential content and spiritual import of those marvelous experiences is unforgettable.)

Fr. Lawrence Edward Tucker, SOLT

Chapter One

MISSION SPIRITUALITY 101

We crossed the border from Brownsville, TX, into Matamoros, MX, at around 7pm with the intention of catching the 8pm bus to Mexico City. It was January, 1988, and this was my first exposure to a developing nation. No amount of preparation would have been useful in helping me make sense of what I was about to experience. Within the distance of a football field, which was the approximate width of the Rio Grande, the differences between the USA and Mexico were so dramatic one might have imagined the two countries were entirely different planets!

The first thing one will notice, apart from the frenetic hustle-bustle of a major border town, is the noise level produced by the constant blare of car horns, people yelling to one another, the whistles of traffic police, and the ever present roar of Tejano music. But this increase in decibel level does not sound like a cacophony, or "bad noise". On the contrary, it is perceived as "happy noise"… the noise of life! The number of young people visible everywhere is just astounding! Unlike in the USA, the institution of the family is very strong and vibrant in Mexico.

The main observable difference however is at the economic level. This dissonance is so great that it is nothing less than shocking. How can there be such poverty within a "stone's throw" of the wealthiest nation in the world?

Poverty was apparent everywhere; the buildings, the streets, the vehicles, the lights… even the signage. I felt like I had gone into a time machine and been transported back to the year 1930. We went into a little luncheonette to get a snack before boarding the bus, and all of the furnishings looked as though they had been lifted from the set of the *Happy Days* TV show... except that all of them were extremely old and falling apart. Even the clothes many people were wearing looked antiquated and appeared to be used articles donated from the USA (*ropa usada*). But the clincher was the number of children weaving in and out of the traffic trying desperately to sell Chiclets. The children appeared to be undernourished and were dressed in worn out, ill-fitting clothing.

At the time, I knew only a few words in Spanish and had no idea what was going on around me. Being so completely "out of the loop" was a strange feeling which morphed very quickly into an uneasy state of frustration. I was utterly fascinated by everything I saw and wanted to connect and converse with the various people we encountered... but that would have to wait. Perhaps in the beginning, this inability to communicate is a good thing... it forces one to be a humble observer of a new culture; a student as opposed to a teacher.

In time, I would come to discover that this particular attitude was crucial to missionary life. Jesus chose to be poor, yet he had so much to give... so much to teach us. Recall that Jesus told his disciples that since he had shared everything with them he could now call them his friends. The missionary must find the humility to learn from the poor or he will never be able to accompany them in authentic Christian friendship.

In the midst of this new and somewhat confusing experience, one thing was certain: there was something uniquely wonderful about this new world. I sensed a greater openness in the people... a warmth and closeness lacking in the "super-developed" USA. The people, in their poverty, radiated a degree of humility I never imagined could even exist. How beautiful and noble they were in their simplicity of heart... in their oneness with Jesus crucified!

The overnight bus-ride to Mexico City (*La Capital*) was like something right out of the Inquisition! The roads had so many bumps and pot holes it seemed like the passengers spent half the trip in mid-air! With the constant noise, impossible seats, and incredibly dangerous roads, I managed (with great difficulty!) to get, at best, an hour of sleep. As my grandmother was fond of saying, it was so torturous, "it would make an innocent man confess!" Don't think the question didn't occur to me... why didn't we take a plane? There were 4 of us; Fr. John McHugh, Alan (a lay missionary), Sister Veronica, and myself (a seminarian). The airfare for 4 adults would have been considerable. But that wasn't the issue. The reason for the bus was much more profound than simple economics.

Fr. John McHugh, the co-founder of our community and the pastor of the Belize mission for 20 years, was a firm believer in *Our Lady's poverty*. The founder of SOLT (*The Society of Our Lady of The Most Holy Trinity*), Fr. James Flanagan, taught that not only did Jesus choose poverty but his blessed mother, having been formed by the Holy Spirit, had already chosen poverty. By imitating our mother's poverty we not only make space for Jesus, but we also create room for the poor. Fr. John, in choosing to take the bus, was showing us that missionary life requires a choice; an "option for the poor" that often involves being one with the poor. The foreign missionary learns and lives the culture of the people he serves and tries to enter into solidarity with them. Had we taken a plane, we would know nothing of the difficulties the poor encounter daily as they travel about in rickety old buses.

"For the Church, the option for the poor is primarily a theological category rather than a cultural, sociological, political or philosophical one. God shows the poor "his first mercy." Inspired by this, the Church has made an option for the poor which is understood as a "special form of primacy in the exercise of Christian charity, to which the whole tradition of the Church bears witness." (EG, 198)

If you ever take a bus from the border of Texas to Mexico City, prepare yourself to be woken up in the middle of the night by the *Imigracion*… the Mexican immigration officials who periodically stop the bus to check the passengers' visas. Everyone must exit the bus, form a line and parade over to a little table where they submit their passport to the official seated there. The official is free to detain anyone for whatever reason he decides. He may not like the way you respond to his questions, or he may feel he needs more time to check out your story; that is, your reason for being in Mexico in the first place. In any case, this interrogation is not a very pleasant experience.

Sure enough, at around 2am our bus pulled into a little truck stop and off to the side we could see a small table with an immigration official seated behind it. When the bus came to a halt the door opened and a second official entered the bus and shouted, "*Papeles!*" (Papers). Everyone was familiar with the drill so we began to exit the bus. Fr John made sure that he was the first of our SOLT group to reach the table. I was thinking, "He put himself in front so he could clear the way for us… how thoughtful". Within seconds, I would have serious doubts regarding this theory!

"***Are you*** a Catholic priest?" asked the official. "Yes", replied Fr. John. "I used to be Catholic", said the official, "but now I'm Protestant". Hearing the official's robust declaration, I sensed instinctively that this might be the end of the road for us. The official continued, "Yeah… I'm so glad to be away from that decrepit and useless Catholic Church. I love being a Protestant!" Then something incredible happened. Fr. John asked the official if he could pose a question. The official responded, "Yes… go ahead. What is your question?"

Fr. John began… "When you were a Catholic, did you believe in the real presence of Jesus in the Eucharist?" The official hesitated and thought for a moment… then responded, "Yes, I did." "No… you didn't," said Fr. John. "Fr. John! What are you doing!" I was saying to myself. At this point, I was sure we would be detained and I was beginning to wonder what our cells would be like. "Yes, I did!" said the official firmly. "No, you didn't!" responded Fr. John, just as firmly. Now I was no longer concerned about the cell I would be getting because I was quite sure we would all be summarily executed somewhere behind the little truck stop building. The official stared Fr. John in the face and with fire in his eyes shouted, "YES, I DID!" Fr. John, without losing a bit of his composure, looked upon the man with the most sincere love and in the gentlest voice imaginable, said the following: "No, you didn't. And I'm going to tell you how I know you didn't. If you did believe that Jesus was truly present in the Eucharist, you would have never left him."

There was complete silence. Everyone was pondering Fr. John's magnificent statement and wondering what would be the net result of this intense exchange. The official motioned to the 3 of us to give him our passports. It seemed as though we were about to be placed under arrest. He now had all 4 passports. He opened them, reviewed them quickly, and without looking up, handed them to Fr. John. Inexplicably, he had given us clearance to travel freely in Mexico!

Back on the bus I questioned Fr. John about this incident, which was only a hair away from being a total disaster. I shared with him how nervous I was and how I had judged him to be reckless and imprudent for having engaged the official as he did. Fr. John said that in time I would come to understand. It was all about how the missionary must follow the Holy Spirit. The mission, he said, depends on the missionary's ability to live in the Spirit. "The mission is here and now!" And with those words he fell asleep. Fr. John had a special gift... he could sleep on a picket fence in the middle of Grand Central Station... during rush hour! I wasn't so lucky. To sleep on that bus, I would have required an I.V. of *AMBIEN*... for each arm! Actually, I was much too preoccupied reflecting on all the amazing things I had witnessed thus far.

That morning we made our connection in Mexico City and were off to Veracruz. The trip went well, but we ran into some road construction delays which meant that our bus probably would not arrive at Veracruz in time to catch the bus to Villahermosa. Once inside the bus station, our fears were confirmed… we missed the bus by 15 minutes. The next bus to Villahermosa was at 10am the following morning. Of course, this meant we would have to spend the night in Veracruz. Finding a place to stay, however, might be problematic… all the motels had "no vacancy" signs displayed. Veracruz is a beautiful, tropical city on the Bay of Campeche (an arm of the Gulf of Mexico), and it's a very popular destination for tourists.

It was time for an impromptu "pow-wow". What should we do? The motel situation seemed pretty desperate. I suggested we begin looking for lodging immediately. Alan and I would explore the main drag in one direction… Fr. John and sister could scope-out the other direction. We would meet back at the terminal in 30 minutes and assess our findings. Alan and sister seemed to be on-board with the idea… Fr. John was not. He said the best thing to do was to find a Church and go to Mass.

I suggested we look for a Church after we find a motel. Fr. John said that given the state of things only God would be able to find us a motel. We acquiesced but remained uncomfortable with Fr. John's plan. We quickly found a Church about 3 blocks away and learned that Mass was about to begin. Fr. John said he wanted to see if he could concelebrate so he made a beeline to the sacristy. A few minutes later he came out of the sacristy and sat next to me. "The priest doesn't believe I'm really a priest!" whispered Fr. John, "He told me that a real priest would never be dressed so poorly!"

A little explanation would be in order here. I already related how Fr. John lived the poverty of Jesus and Mary. What I failed to mention was that, consequently, Fr. John was overflowing with boundless joy! When I first met Fr. John I didn't know what to make of him. He was not like any other priest I had ever met. He was so filled with joy that it actually made me uncomfortable. He seemed to live in a carefree world where everything was possible and there was nothing to fear.

At first, I didn't even realize he was a priest. His black pants were faded and utterly worn out. He was wearing a black clerical shirt unbuttoned at the neck with the plastic, white-collar insert sticking out of the shirt pocket that was still intact... the other pocket was torn and dangling. The shirt was so old it had turned gray with the years and was frayed all around the collar. (I wouldn't be surprised if he had received it as an ordination gift 40 years earlier!)

Atop his head was a dark blue, wool Navy hat, and on his feet was a common pair of black shoes that were so scuffed and damaged The Salvation Army would have thrown them in the trash. The general impression he made was that of a happy-go-lucky vagabond. But by the end of our Trans-Mexico excursion to Belize, I would come to know Fr. John as he truly was... a holy missionary priest.

This being the case, I still couldn't understand how the priest in the sacristy failed to recognize the humility of his brother priest. Nevertheless, I wanted to enter the sacristy and speak with him on Fr. John's behalf. Humbly accepting this rejection, Fr. John said he wasn't offended and asked me to simply pray for the priest. But it was difficult to focus during Mass, knowing that the celebrant thought the man sitting next to me was impersonating a priest (given his un-priestly attitude, it was far more likely that the parish priest was the impostor!). Perhaps he imagined that Sister Veronica was impersonating a religious... and that the four of us were outlaws on-the-run after pulling off a major heist of some kind! In any case, the arrogance that was so vividly on display in this incident is just one of the many insults the poor deal with regularly.

After Mass we left the Church and as we were descending a long series of steps that went from the entrance of the Church to street level, I saw a man and a woman standing together on the sidewalk and they appeared to be studying us. They walked in our direction and met us as we reached the final step. "You're American missionaries?" they inquired. "Yes", responded Fr. John. "You're traveling and need a place to stay tonight?" "Yes!" exclaimed Fr. John. "We own a hotel one block from the terminal and we would like to give you free lodging for the night. Also, today, is my wife's birthday and we are having a big party at our house. We would like you to join us there for dinner."

We looked at one another wondering if we heard this incredible invitation correctly. Perhaps under the influence of fasting and sleep deprivation we heard something we really wanted to hear but was not actually said... a sort of auditory mirage. Fr. John, however, knew immediately what was going on... God had answered our prayers! Speaking for our group, Fr. John gratefully accepted the invitation and we walked a couple of blocks to their home.

The house was buzzing with excitement! Balloons and birthday decorations were everywhere. It was quite a family reunion with at least 40 people in attendance. The buffet was groaning with food. You could choose Mexican or American... the options were endless (a "dream come true" for starving missionaries!). Some of the guests actually lived in the USA and were visiting for the occasion. As a bonus prize, the Super Bowl was being shown on the family TV and we had the pleasure of enjoying it with our new friends.

After dinner, we were taken to the hotel and shown our rooms. We gathered together for evening prayer in one of the rooms and gave heartfelt thanks to God. Clearly, we had so much to be grateful for! Not one of us ever questioned how this mysterious couple knew so much about us because all of us could sense that, ultimately, it was God who had rescued us. We apologized to Fr.

John for doubting his plan. He said things always go better if you put God first. "That's how the poor live," he said, "They have insight into living the Gospel that many people better off no longer have". Fr. John was teaching us how to *live* the Gospel because he realized that the best way to communicate the Gospel is to live it!

"We need to remember that all religious teaching ultimately has to be reflected in the teacher's way of life, which awakens the assent of the heart by its nearness, love and witness." (EG, 42)

Fr. Lawrence Edward Tucker, SOLT

Chapter Two

OUT TO THE PERIPHERY

When Fr. Flanagan asked me to help Fr. John in Belize, I really didn't know what he was talking about because I had no idea that the word "Belize" was the name of a country. It wasn't until he explained how Belize was formerly British Honduras that I began to understand his request. Trusting in God and putting aside my natural caution, I accepted the challenge. Having left the seminary to enter into formation with SOLT, this assignment to Belize would give me not only exposure to the SOLT family/team charism, but also hands-on experience of trans-cultural mission.

As I began to get some things together for an excursion to a place I never heard of, I found myself reflecting on my life to see if the Lord had somehow been preparing me for this leap in faith. I quickly realized that he had in fact been forming me for this beautiful way of life. It never really registered with me, but I already had a very rich trans-cultural experience under my belt.

My Family moved to Hawaii when I was 16 years old because my father, an iron worker at the time, was offered a once in a lifetime opportunity to be part of a big construction project in Honolulu. We rented a little house on the windward side of the main island of Oahu, 3 blocks from the beach in a town named Kailua. I enrolled in the 11th grade at Kailua High School and quickly made some friends; all of them native Hawaiians.

My friends taught me a great deal about traditional Hawaiian culture. They showed me how to make poi as well as how to relate well with the native Hawaiians. I developed a great admiration for the Hawaiians and their long standing customs. One of the things I found disturbing, however, was the poverty of the native people. All of the Hawaiians I knew were poor. Their homes were usually overcrowded, rundown shacks that were very poorly furnished. Why is it that indigenous people are always at the bottom of the socioeconomic ladder? They're gifted human beings and yet they always seem to be left behind. Look at the Native Americans, the Aztecs of Mexico, the Mayans of Guatemala, the Inca of Peru, the Guarani of Paraguay… to name just a handful! Pope Francis has something to say in this regard:

> *"Today everything comes under the laws of competition and the survival of the fittest, where the powerful feed upon the powerless. As a consequence masses of people find themselves excluded and marginalized: without work, without possibilities, without any means of escape." (EG, 53)*

These feelings of exclusion, or better yet, outright rejection, are not known to bring out the best in people; it's hard to relate well when one is treated like an outcast… in one's own native land! During my family's time in Hawaii I was devouring Scripture. Every day I would do about an hour of what is called *Lectio Divina* (at the time, of course, I didn't know there was a name for the prayerful reading of Scripture). I had fallen in love with the Word of God to such a degree that I would take my paperback copy of the New Testament with me whenever I went on an outing. One evening, David (a Hawaiian friend) and I went into Waikiki for a stroll along the beach (Waikiki is popular not only with tourists… the native people enjoy its beauty as well). As you walk the beach, you will generally see luaus with hula dancers and Hawaiians singing traditional songs in their native language, accompanied by a local musician strumming away on a Ukulele.

The sun was setting and the beach was relatively calm as we sauntered along. I asked David if he ever thought about leaving the islands to live on the mainland. He looked at me as if I had just proposed something akin to apostasy. "I could never leave my ocean or my mountains!" he said firmly... as though issuing an edict. As we continued walking I noticed 2 gargantuan Hawaiian men coming towards us. David turned to me and whispered, "These guys are *mokes*. Let me handle them... don't say a word." I was perplexed? The tone of David's voice led me to believe the 2 behemoths approaching us were dangerous. But David was only 5'2" and weighed in at around 100 pounds. How could he possibly fend off these mammoth Hawaiians? This was shaping up to be a replay of *David and Goliath*... only in this case there were 2 Goliaths! I gripped my New Testament a little tighter and sent out a quick "S.O.S." to the living God.

When they reached us they positioned themselves directly in front of us blocking our path (being the size of NFL linemen they also blocked our view!). One of them looked down menacingly at David and in something just short of a growl, said, "Who are you?" David told him his name... along with the names of his parents, his relatives, his family history, the town he was from, etc. Then pointing to me, the moke said, "Who's da *Haole?*" "Bruddah," David said, "he is my friend. He's not a tourist. He lives in Kailua and goes to Kailua high school. He's a good person, bruddah... he eats poi and he prays. See the book in his hand... that's the Bible!"

They must have been satisfied with David's answer because without saying another word they continued on their way. "What's a *moke?*" I asked David. He said that mokes were angry Hawaiians, usually unemployed, who went around looking for trouble. They liked to intimidate and harass foreigners who showed "disrespect" for their island or their people. "And what's a *Haole?*" I asked. "You!" said David, "people that look like you!" "Mokes," I thought, "what a pathetic waste of human potential!" Does the Church have anything to say about all this? Let's listen to Pope Francis:

"The poor and the poorer peoples are accused of violence, yet without equal

opportunities the different forms of aggression and conflict will find a fertile terrain for growth and will eventually explode." (EG: 59)

As I continued to reflect on my life I dredged up a number of other adventure experiences but none that involved an entirely different culture. I use the word "adventure" in the strict sense where it means a venturing forth from the familiar. Surely, there are missionaries who are wanderlusts and who seek adventure for its own sake. But the adventure of mission is much more authentic than the rush one might get from something like Bungee Jumping. The mission adventure comes directly out of the Gospel... "He who loses his life for my sake, *and that of the Gospel,* will find it!" (Mt 10:39).

"...all of us are called to take part in this new missionary 'going forth'... to go forth from our own comfort zone in order to reach all the peripheries in need of the light of the Gospel." (EG, 20)

Fr. Flanagan once shared something very beautiful on the subject of "adventure". I was driving him to a parish in South Texas where he was scheduled to celebrate Mass and the subject of our new mission in New Guinea came up. I said that whoever went there would be in for an amazing adventure. Fr. Jim replied, "It will be nothing compared to the adventure we are about to enter into when we get to this parish... the wondrous adventure of the Paschal Mystery!"

Convinced that the Lord had been preparing me for this day, I continued packing. "Mosquito Repellant"... CHECK! "Hiking Boots"... CHECK! "Malaria Pills"... CHECK! "Sunscreen"... CHECK! "Spanish Language"... OOOPS!" I would have to work on that one. Actually, the official language of Belize is English but the people of Benque favor Spanish because the town is on the border of Guatemala... a Spanish speaking country.

I already shared in the INTRODUCTION the exuberant welcome I received when I arrived at *Our Lady of Mount Carmel* mission. With that in mind, it should be apparent how out of character the following snippet of Benque history is. Before SOLT, the mission had been staffed by the Jesuits. Late one night someone broke into the rectory and, using a machete, murdered the Jesuit pastor while he was working at his desk. This crime was never officially solved, but solved or unsolved it was still very difficult for the Bishop to decide what to do with the mission following a traumatic event of this nature.

As providence would have it, not long after this tragedy the Bishop of Belize was in Missouri and met Fr. Flanagan at a Church social. They discussed the mission and Fr. Flanagan assured the Bishop that SOLT would be happy to serve in Benque. The rest is history. The mission now has an Elementary School, a High School, and a Junior College. The SOLT team also takes care of the mission parish of *San Martin de Porres* in the Guatemalan border town of *Melchor de Mencos*. This mission is just across the Mopan River from Benque and includes 30 Mayan villages spread across *El Petén Jungle* (home of the famous Mayan archeological site… TIKAL).

The arrival of a new missionary in Benque, therefore, was not something unusual. Nevertheless, there would always be a gathering of local people to extend an exceptionally warm welcome to the newcomer. After a friendly conversation with the townspeople, I climbed the outdoor staircase and went into the rectory. In order to fully understand what this particular rectory was like one must recall everything I have already shared regarding Fr. John. To say that the rectory was a model of simplicity would be an enormous understatement. To put it in the most rudimentary terms, the only furnishings in the house were those that were absolutely essential. My bedroom had a few shelves and a bed made of hardwood boards with a complementary 2" thick piece of foam rubber that served as a mattress. Fr. John's room was even more Spartan… he had some shelves and a hammock (I would come to understand the rationale behind the choice of a hammock!).

There's really no point in continuing to describe the interior of the rectory because the fact is… it was so barren it would have made an Amish home seem like the Waldorf Astoria! The entire house was raised on pilings about 12 feet above the ground, which explains why one of the redeeming features of this old, dilapidated jungle cabin was its side porch. Since the rectory was on a little hill, the porch provided a very enjoyable view of things. One of the more impressive sights was a completely excavated Mayan temple named *XUNANTUNICH*. Also, it was not uncommon to see at close range colorful Toucans, Quetzals, and flocks of beautiful Parrots. Benque is located in a hilly, tropical rain forest (otherwise known as a jungle!) and the natural environment is teeming with life.

After a dinner of rice and beans, Fr. John and I, along with Alan and a couple of young Peace Corps volunteers, went out on the porch to unwind and watch the sunset. The volunteers and I began to discuss philosophy asking one another about our favorite philosophers. One said his favorite was the Danish philosopher, Soren Kierkegaard *(Fear and Trembling,* 1843*)*. Another liked a French thinker named Gabriel Marcel *(The Mystery of Being,* 1951*)*. I said I enjoyed the writings of the Jewish philosopher, Martin Buber *(I and Thou,* 1923*)*. Then I turned to Fr. John, who was at the far end of the porch stretched out in an airy rope hammock… "Fr. John, who is your favorite philosopher?" He gazed out at the tree line for a moment, then turned his eyes in our direction and said, "You know… I have to say that, well… my favorite philosopher is Popeye! Really… I mean it! Think about it… Popeye was an American existentialist! Remember what he always said, *'I am what I am and that's all that I am … I'm Popeye the Sailorman.'* You see how he embraces the limitations of his being… and how clear and strong he is in his identity!"

Leave it to Fr. John to discover the greatest philosopher of the 20th century… a cartoon character named Popeye! We were laughing so hard I thought we would wake up the Mayan rulers buried at Xunantunitch! Even Fr. John was laughing! Of course, that was the whole idea… Fr. John wanted to show us how to relax and enjoy the simplicity of the mission. This was a new world and to understand it one would need a new hermeneutic of poverty and humility. Basically, he was telling us to leave our stressful baggage behind so that we could enter into the simple joy of the gospel.

We "hit the hay" (in my case, the hardwood boards!) at around 11pm. Before retiring to my 6'x 10' cubicle/sweatbox, Fr. John asked me if I would do him a favor in the morning and drive into Belize City to retrieve a load of donated school books that were waiting for us on the dock. I said I would be happy to go and asked who would be joining me. Fr. John explained that unfortunately there was no one available to go with me but that he would give me a map and I would be fine. "Great, Fr. John," I said, "see you in the morning." "Si Dios quiere!" (if God wills it) replied Fr. John.

This was my first night sleeping in the mission and I was wondering what it would be like. With all the excitement and the unusual sounds of the jungle (not to mention the sweltering heat!) would I be able to sleep at all? I guess Popeye was right… human beings do have very real limitations; I was asleep as soon as my head hit the foam rubber! As desirous as this healthful "syncope and collapse" was, however, it was too good to last.

In the middle of the night I felt an itch on the left side of my face. I went to scratch my cheek and my hand touched something that definitely was not me! There was a giant cockroach attached to my face and apparently it was eating me alive! My first impression was that it was some kind of mutant because it was at least 5x's the size of a normal cockroach, and its appearance was so "alien" it could have come out of central casting for a science fiction movie! I would soon learn that creatures in the rainforest grow much bigger than they would anywhere else.

Now, I know what you're thinking… you never heard of a man-eating cockroach. Well neither did I… until I woke up that night with one chewing on my face (of course… a "man-nibbling" cockroach would be more precise. But I'm trying to express the impression that such things make on a person going through a profound *Culture Shock*). After tearing the beast off my cheek and crushing it underfoot, I searched my cubicle to see if there were any more of these monstrous insects lurking in the night. Satisfied that the room was now safe, my heart-rate returned to normal and I went back to sleep.

About an hour later, I was rudely awakened a second time. Again, it was something utterly gross… but a bit more familiar. A big rat scurried across my bare chest! I jumped up, hit the light and there he was… cowering in the corner; AHA! The proverbial, "*cornered rat!*" I had been hearing about him my whole life and now we were face to face… "Not a good thing," I thought. So I stomped my foot and he scampered under the bed. I flipped up the entire bed and watched him disappear through a hole in one of the mahogany floor boards. It didn't take a rocket scientist to realize that the hole was his means of entry into the room, so I stuffed it with one of my T-shirts, switched off the light and went back to bed; all the while trying to imagine what type of hideous jungle creature was at that moment preparing to mount the next major offensive against this terrified new resident of their *"Little Shop of Horrors!"*

Believe it or not, despite the relentless attacks by the viciously territorial occupants of the rectory/menagerie, I slept very well. The first thing I did upon rising was inspect my room and try to find out how that "weaponized" roach got in. I couldn't figure it out and was about to give up when I sat on the bed and noticed something. The space between the bottom of the door and the floor was very small except in one spot where a floor board was warped. At that particular spot the clearance was about an inch. I wouldn't have to worry about Hannibal's elephants getting through, but it was a veritable Khyber Pass for a hostile band of marauding cockroaches! I rolled up a bath towel into the shape of a tube and laid it along the bottom of the door... Perfect! Problem solved.

Actually, one home improvement remained to be implemented. After my night in the "Hanoi Hilton", I finally grasped the wisdom of using a hammock. It's very simple... a hammock is at least 3' off the floor. A rat would have to put on his NIKE'S to get up there... and a cockroach would have had to be trained by *The Flying Wallendas* (a high-wire circus act) to successfully negotiate either of the 2 ropes from which the hammock is suspended.

After retiring from my brief career as a pest exterminator, I went into the kitchen and showed Fr. John the big red welt on my face caused by a cockroach the size of a mouse! He didn't seem very impressed. He said the real danger was if a vampire bat infected with rabies were to get into the room and bite you as you slept. Their bite is so gentle you would never feel it... and the marks they leave are so tiny you probably wouldn't notice them in the morning. By the time you showed symptoms, the disease would already be beyond remedy. "Rabies is a horrible death!" he lamented. Only Fr. John could make a person feel good about having been savagely attacked by a man-eating, mutant cockroach!

The amazing thing is, none of this repulsed me or made me want to pack and head for the airport. On the contrary, I was fascinated by the interesting creatures and the unusual living conditions. But the deeper "hook" that had found its way into my heart was the warmth and transparency of the humble people who had so graciously welcomed me into their lives the day before (if a person were to open their heart and extend a similar welcome to Jesus... that person would surely become a saint!).

As I waited on line at the local grocery store, sporting a big mark on the side of my face but feeling like the luckiest person in the world for not having contracted rabies, I began to think about the 2 ½ hour trip into Belize City. I'd read there are more Jaguars per square mile in the Maya Mountains of Belize than in the Amazon Basin. Maybe I would be lucky enough to catch a glimpse of one crossing the Great Western Highway (sounds like a big road. It wasn't at the time… only one lane in each direction, and a couple of sections were unpaved).

Having spent a few Belize dollars on some provisions for my trip, I returned to the rectory to get the all-important map. Fr. John, with a somewhat out-of-character concerned look on his face, met me at the door and asked me to come in and sit down because there was something we needed to discuss… "Manatee Highway, that's the old road that goes south from Belize City to Dangriga, is notorious for having bandits," he said, "You have to be very careful on your return trip because it's so easy to get confused and end up on the road to Dangriga. Please be sure to follow the map."

I assured Fr. John I had no desire to visit with the bandits and I would certainly be careful and stick with the map. He gave me a blessing and I headed out on my first official mission assignment. I have to say, I wasn't nervous… I was very excited! I had seen enough on the Trans-Mexico bus trip to know that God always goes with his missionaries to guide and protect them. I would find the dock, load up the books, and bring them back safely to Benque. No problem… mission accomplished!

The trip to Belize City went very well. Belize City itself was a bit confusing, but the map Fr. John made was excellent and led me directly to the dock. Because of the intense midday tropical heat, it took almost an hour to load all the books by myself. Although the truck was now filled with an assortment of used elementary school textbooks, in my mind, understanding the value of education, I was transporting nothing less than *King Tut's Treasure*… and I was feeling very good about the whole thing!

Entering the cab of the pickup with a great sense of accomplishment, I took a long, deep breath in preparation for the next leg of the journey... the victorious trip back to the mission. "Now... where did I put that map?" I asked myself. Truth be told, I had no idea what I did with it! I was so excited when I arrived at the dock that I completely lost track of the map. I looked everywhere... but it was gone. Perhaps it found its way into one of the boxes? Maybe... but more likely the wind had gotten hold of it and deposited it into the canal. The map I assured Fr. John I would "stick with"... the key to getting back to the mission safely... was probably on its way out to sea!

Was I worried? No... not really. I figured the same God who got me to the dock safely would somehow get me back to the mission. Also, I had been making mental notes of various landmarks on the way in and I felt they would be good enough to guide me back to Benque. Putting a little more faith in my mental notes than in the mercy of God, I put the truck in gear and with false bravado working overtime, launched out into the unknown.

The return trip was going quite well until things started to look consistently unfamiliar. "Wow... I definitely don't remember this narrow stretch of dirt road winding through dense jungle!" I murmured nervously to myself. Being the only vehicle on the road, it wasn't long before I was convinced that I had indeed made a wrong turn and was now on the infamous road to Dangriga... which also meant I was probably on my way to a "close encounter" with the bandits!

Was I worried now? YES... I was *very* worried! I began to wonder, "what could be worse than this?" Well it was as if the Lord heard me and responded, "I can think of something!" Immediately the truck's engine began to spit and cough... and then it stopped entirely. The gas gauge said it all... the truck was out of gas. My situation at this point was so bad it was almost comical! As the saying goes, I didn't know whether to laugh or cry! I decided to do neither. Instead… I would register a complaint with the Lord. In a silent, heartfelt way I said something like this… "Lord, I'm angry. This makes no sense at all. My first day as a missionary… my very first assignment… and I'm lost, out of gas, and about to fall into the hands of bandits! Is this supposed to be funny? I'm not laughing, Lord! Think about it, Lord… this is not at all cost effective. What a waste of training… you haven't gotten any return out of me yet! Think of the many years of missionary service I could give you."

In desperation, I got out of the truck, shut the door and looked around. I was truly in that famous place called… *The Middle of Nowhere!* In my case, the "middle of nowhere" was a narrow dirt road with tall, thick jungle on either side. Having expressed my feelings and regained a bit of my composure, I knew what I had to do. It was now time to pray… "Lord, I don't know what you can do here… but I know you can do anything you want. Please help me!" Suddenly, I heard a vehicle coming from the direction I had been heading, that is, from up ahead where I imagined the bandits to be. I couldn't see the vehicle because I had run out of gas on a long curve. I assumed the vehicle approaching would be the bandits or someone associated with them.

From what I could tell, I had about a minute to take some evasive action. But what could I do? The first thing that came to mind was to hide in the jungle. Then I remembered a little story Fr. John shared with me on the Trans-Mexico trip. I had asked Fr. John how big do Boa Constrictors get. He told me a true story about a man who took his eight-year-old son with him into the jungle to collect "leña" (firewood). He told the boy, "sit down on that log over there and I'll be back in a few minutes." When the man returned the boy was gone… and so was the "log"!

Factoring in many other things I heard about the perils of the jungle, I decided to take my chances with the bandits. Perhaps I could offer them the truck along with the books in exchange for my life. I thought I was quite brilliant coming up with that idea… until I realized how patently ridiculous it was. Why would a self-respecting bandit have to bargain with anyone? By definition, a bandit is someone who takes whatever he wants… at gunpoint! He's an armed robber… not a shopper looking for a good deal! Besides, what in the world would they want with hundreds of used elementary school textbooks? If they were literate they probably wouldn't be bandits. Fine…I won't try to bargain with them.

Would it be possible to scare them in some way? Maybe I could say I was related to some powerful person. No… that wouldn't work either. It would only encourage them to hold me for ransom. Perhaps I would get lucky and the bandits would turn out to be a troupe of bungling misfits similar to the *Over the Hill Gang*. Right… dream on! The way my luck was going they would probably be more qualified than *Billy the kid and the Regulators*! With that scenario rolling around in my head, I finally realized I was in God's hands and there was nothing I could do other than to trust in him. I went and stood in front of the truck to meet my destiny head-on.

As the vehicle came around the bend I could see that it was one of those classic old jeeps without a roof. I could also see that the only person in it was the driver. As the jeep got closer, I realized that the driver was probably not a bandit at all. He appeared to be a proper Englishman in Khaki shorts and a matching short-sleeved shirt. I knew there were still some British in Belize, but I was not ready to let my guard down just yet. After all, this fellow could be working with the bandits as their scout. Maybe it was his job to determine who I was and if I was armed, then report back to the gang.

The Jeep pulled right up to me and in a very cheerful voice, but without a British accent, the driver said, "You're out of gas?" Utterly confused, I responded in a cautious tone, "Yes." "I have a five-gallon can of gas here," said the driver of the jeep, "Mind if I put it in your tank?" I was so stunned I was truly speechless, "No," I replied sheepishly... still trying to figure out what was going on. I stood there motionless as he poured the gas into my truck's gas tank. I was standing so completely still I must have resembled a possum playing dead... while this mysterious individual was at the rear of the truck humming a cheerful tune and apparently enjoying the whole experience! We were like a study in contrasts. When he was finished he jumped back into the jeep and said, "OK... you're all set!" "Thanks", was all I could manage... given the stupefied condition I was in.

He drove away in the direction I had come from... and I decided, for some strange reason, to continue forward in the direction he had just come from. Actually, the fellow in the jeep radiated such authenticity that somehow I knew it would be a good idea to travel in that direction or he would have said something. It turned out to be an excellent decision because within less than ½ a mile there was a little dirt road on the right complete with a sign displaying an arrow and the words... WESTERN HIGHWAY!

After arriving in Benque, I parked the truck at Deacon Cal's house, crossed the street and went directly into the Church to thank the Lord for having saved me from what could have been a calamitous experience. As I entered the beautiful old mission Church of *Our Lady of Mount Carmel,* I was surprised to see Fr. John in the front pew. "Hello, Fr. John, I'm back," I whispered. Fr. John jumped up, turned around, and in a very excited voice said, "Larry! I'm so happy to see you! How'd it go?" I gave him a blow-by-blow account of the entire journey; how I arrived at the dock, lost the map, ended up on the road to Dangriga, ran out of gas, and was assisted by a very mysterious "good samaritan" who arrived right on cue.

"Larry," he began, "you have no idea what really happened today. About 3 hours after you left I heard that bandits had set up

shop on the Western Highway. The map I gave you would have led you right into their trap. I was worried sick, so I went before the Blessed Sacrament and was begging Jesus and Mary to protect you." "So you're saying it was good I lost the map?" I said. Fr. John continued, "Actually, Larry… I don't think you lost the map. I think the Lord took it from you, knowing it would no longer be helpful. And by getting "lost" on the road to Dangriga, you actually went around the bandit roadblock on the perimeter of Belize City. Do you see how the Lord was with you?"

"Yes, Fr. John… I'm beginning to understand," I replied. "Now tell me about this mysterious "good samaritan", said Fr. John, "Did he speak much?" "No… he said very little," I responded, "but he was relaxed and cheerful." "And did you speak much to him?" questioned Fr. John. "Three words; *yes… no…* and, *thanks*," I replied. "Good", said Fr. John, "I'm glad." "Larry", he said, "listen to me… that man was an angel. That's right… an angel! In the missions, Larry, we work with the angels; they're part of our team! You will see… they will come to your aid time and time again. Without their help we could never succeed in any mission."

"Wow… how absolutely wonderful!" I thought to myself, "I think I'm going to like it here… ANGELS! This is awesome!" In a period of 24 hours I had been assaulted by a bizarre creature who really belonged in Dante's *Inferno*, and later, in a separate incident, was rescued by way of a personal encounter with an angel who would have been very much at home in Dante's *Paradiso!* I was sold… missionary life was just incomparable! But the most exciting dimension of the whole experience was how much I was learning.

When I arrived at the mission I was somewhat "puffed-up" thinking I was taking on a very difficult missionary challenge. I pictured myself as some kind of heroic figure… like a modern day Francis Xavier. What I discovered, however, was quite the opposite. It turns out that I wasn't doing the mission at all. If anything, I was more or less in the way! It's the Lord who does the mission... he's the real missionary! I forgot to gas up the truck, misplaced the map, and ended up lost in the jungle (at least I'm consistently imperfect!). Nevertheless... the Lord pulled victory out of the jaws of defeat.

The main thing the missionary must learn is to simply get out of the way! The Lord is on fire with missionary joy and there are so many things he wants to do ("I have come to set a fire on the earth... how I long to see it kindled!" Luke 12: 49). The missionary must realize that it is really Jesus who is doing the mission... the missionary is just tagging along because Jesus doesn't like to work alone. Without this spiritual perspective, discouragement would set in like a cold, damp fog. I was beginning to understand what Fr. John said about the missionary living in the Spirit. If we are humble and sincere, the Lord will do in us what he did at the wedding feast of Cana. He will take the "water" of our feeble human efforts and transform them into the "wine" of an abundant harvest!

"Though it is true that this mission demands great generosity on our part, it would be wrong to see it as a heroic individual undertaking, for it is first and foremost the Lord's work surpassing anything we can see and understand. Jesus is 'the first and greatest evangelizer.' In every activity of evangelization, the primacy always belongs to God, who has called us to cooperate with him and who leads us on by the power of his Spirit. This conviction enables us to maintain a spirit of joy in the midst of a task so demanding and challenging that it engages our entire life." (EG, 12)

Chapter Three

BEGIN WITH THE POOR

Leaving the mission in Belize was difficult. I made many friends among the people we served, and it was not easy to say goodbye. But it was time to continue with priestly formation, so I bought a one-way ticket to Houston, TX, and began to pack my belongings. I decided to bequeath my hiking boots to the *jardinero* (gardener) who took care of the Church property. He was an older man who spent the entire day in a crouched position cutting the grass with a machete. After 5 days or so, he would reach the end of the property and then start the whole process over again. One day, he invited me into his large family's extremely humble home. It was a small, wooden cabin with a grand total of 2 rooms. He took something off the wall and handed it to me. It was a plaque the British had given him for having served as their guide in the exploration of the impenetrable Maya Mountains.

This, along with many other memories, raced through my head as I waited in the airport for my flight to be called. I thought about the unique skills and extraordinary knowledge our humble gardener possessed. He was an absolute master of the jungle and was considered by his peers to be the best guide in the country. After a number of disastrous attempts with less talented guides, I found his guidance was the key factor regarding the success of a critically important expedition. He knew all the dangerous plants and animals. He knew what things could be eaten and what things should be left alone. For example: fruit that is on the ground beneath a tree should not be eaten. Very often poisonous snakes drink from the grounded fruit and leave a trace of venom behind in the process.

Then there's the question of which trail to use. The Tapir is a mammal similar to a cow and is the largest animal in the rain forest. Due to their XL size (up to 650 lbs) they leave a relatively big path through the jungle, and it's very tempting to walk along it. But there is a down side that one should consider: jaguars love to eat tapirs and they usually lie in wait along their trails (as Shakespeare said in *The Merchant of Venice*, "all that glisters is not gold.").

One bit of jungle info that I found truly amazing… one of those "tricks of the trade" known only by the master guides that could easily mean the difference between life and death… had to do with the deadly poisonous *Barba Amarilla* (Yellow Jaw). This snake is to Central America what the notorious *Black Mamba* is to Central Africa… a feared killer! The Barba Amarilla is a *Fer da Lance* (literally: iron of the lance, or, spearhead) and is commonly referred to as the ultimate pit viper. The problem with this snake is that unlike most snakes this one is territorial and aggressive. If you surprise or disturb one, there is a good chance it will attack you.

On one occasion, I was preparing to hike out to a Mayan village in Guatemala, and my guide handed me a machete, saying that I would need it if I were attacked by a Yellow Jaw. He added that there was a particular way the machete should be used in the event of an attack. The Yellow Jaw, he explained, which can grow up to 8' long, attacks with such force that it will appear to be flying. If you strike it with the sharp side of the blade the head will come off and probably land somewhere on your body… in which case you would be mortally wounded. It's vital, therefore, to strike the snake with the blunt side of the blade.

"Honestly!" I thought, "what are the chances I would actually remember such a counter-intuitive tactic in the midst of a surprise attack by an 8' long 'flying' snake?" By the grace of God, I was never attacked by one. In fact, the only time I ever saw a Yellow Jaw was when I was driving one afternoon from Benque to Belmopan (the capital of Belize). I saw something drifting across the road that seemed to be around 8' long with the front half about 3' off the ground. I thought it was a reed or a piece of palm so I slowed down not wanting to hit it. When I came closer I could see that it was a Yellow Jaw. The point of all this is not simply to share some interesting jungle facts but to highlight the specialized knowledge and unique skill-set of an amazing man who helped the British achieve an extremely important objective, yet he and his family were still living in abject poverty.

Perhaps in his humility he wanted nothing more than to serve his country. Maybe… but I suspect that this was a classic case of the poor being under-rewarded for their gifts and contributions to society. Sadly, this tendency to neglect and exploit the poor has been a dark shadow haunting the human family throughout its entire history. No doubt, this is one of the main reasons Jesus gave the poor a special, foundational place in his ministry ("Go and report to John… the poor have the Gospel preached to them." Matthew 11: 4-5). Whereas man, weakened by sin, has abandoned them, God would embrace his poor children and bestow the fullness of his Spirit on them through the gift of the Gospel. This super-natural manifestation of love would be the sign that the *Reign of God* was in our midst!

> *"If the whole Church takes up this missionary impulse, she has to go forth to everyone without exception. But to whom should she go first? When we read the Gospel we find a clear indication: not so much our friends and wealthy neighbors, but above all the poor and the sick, those who are usually despised and overlooked, 'those who cannot repay you' (Lk 14:14)." (EG, 48)*

The Belize City airport is bigger now, but in those days it was much smaller… about the size of a professional basketball court.

There was no seating… everyone just stood around and waited for their flight to be called, at which point you were led out to the tarmac. As I stood there reminiscing, gazing out the window at the beautiful Palm trees swaying in the breeze, I caught a glimpse of what appeared to be an American tourist entering the terminal. How could I tell he was a tourist? There were certain tell-tale signs: a straw hat, white shorts, a flower shirt, a sunburn, and 2 cameras hanging from his neck… all good indicators of that not so rare species known as the American tourist!

As the man came through the glass doors and into the building he was immediately met by a youngster toting a shoeshine kit. "Sir… can I shine your shoes?" he humbly asked. Evidently the tourist was in a vile mood. "NO!" he yelled, "Get away from me… I've already wasted too much money in this rotten country of yours! Get out of my way!" I couldn't believe what I was seeing. Clearly… that innocent boy should never have been treated so harshly. The destitute shoeshine kids are as much a part of the airport as the planes… only the kids are a bit more reliable!

I turned away from this unsettling scene, looked out the window, then closed my eyes and began to pray. I prayed for the tourist… that he would find peace and realize the harm he was doing. I prayed for the youngster… that he would bounce back from that verbal assault and not develop a hatred for Americans. When I finished my little interior prayer I opened my eyes, turned around, and who do you think was standing right in front of me? None other than the boy who had just been treated so horribly by the American tourist! "Sir… can… can I… shine your shoes?" he said in a halting, gun-shy way. I looked at him… looked down at my shoes… then, with a puzzled look on my face, looked back at the boy. "Can you shine suede shoes?" I asked. The boy dropped down on one knee to take a closer look at the shoes, then, with the confidence of a noble prize-winning scientist, looked up at me and with consummate assurance said, "Yes sir… I can put a beautiful shine on those shoes."

There was no way I was going to disappoint this brave little guy who at that point was practically suffering from *PTSD*. Heck… if I were barefoot I would have let him shine my feet! I have to admit his confident reply made me very curious… maybe he knew something I didn't know about suede shoes? Perhaps there was a method that only the poor children in the Belize City airport knew about. Maybe they were in possession of a secret formula derived from some rare tropical plant or animal? "Good", I said, "Go ahead… I'd like to see how this works."

Of course my gut instinct told me it was impossible (and completely unnecessary!) to shine suede shoes, but the outcome of this experiment was irrelevant. The only thing that mattered was that the Lord had sent me one of his wounded lambs to be healed and consoled. The boy took some sort of mysterious concoction out of his even more mysterious kit, then, with the precision of an alchemist, carefully chose just the right piece of cloth for this particular application. Indeed, I was rather impressed with the whole ritual until the actual shining process was underway full tilt. Small fragments of suede began flying off in every direction like shrapnel! I'm not sure what was going on in the little fellow's head… did he think suede was some kind of unwanted moss that grew on leather shoes and it was his job to remove it? I didn't know… but this much I did know; he was most certainly removing it!

When he was finished destroying my shoes he looked up at me and with a real sense of pride said, "how's that for a shine!" True… there was evidence of a shine where there had been none before… regardless of how inappropriate that was. I thanked him and gave him more than twice the going rate. As I was settling the bill with this little noble laureate, another shoeshine kid arrived on the scene and said, "Sir… that's not a shine. I can put a real shine on those shoes." This second expert was just as professional as the first, although he seemed to have more of an entrepreneurial/competitive spirit about him.

By the time the *"Steve Jobs"* of the shoeshine industry was done with the shoes they were practically free of that horrible "growth" (a shoeshine kid's worst nightmare!) commonly known as suede. It took only 2 more kids to completely denude the shoes and return them to their original, pristine state of pure, unadulterated leather. In total... 4 shoeshine kids had taken a whack at shining the unshinable shoes! And each one was given his special "differential bonus" for having stepped up to the plate and taken on an impossible challenge.

All of us were laughing and enjoying the silliness of the whole exercise. Then they began to share with me what it was like to work in the airport and the many difficulties they faced daily. I realized that this was a privileged moment so I continued to listen to them, occasionally asking a question. At some point, one of the boys announced, "Sir, you don't have to stand... I'm going to get you a chair." "Wait!" I said, "Where are you going to get a chair?" "I'm going into the offices over there and take one," he replied casually. "No... no don't... you'll get in trouble!" Thirty seconds later he was back with a chair and insisted I sit on it... so I did; all the while expecting an airport official would spot me and accuse me of having stolen the chair.

When I heard my flight called I told the young businessmen that the first ever *"Shoeshine Workers Convention"* was now officially ended. They offered to carry my little backpack to the door that leads to the tarmac, but I suggested something else. "In thanksgiving for this providential meeting we had here today, could I ask you to say a little prayer?" Well, they completely misunderstood what I was proposing; probably because I didn't express myself clearly. I was simply asking them to pray sometime... not for me... but for the sake of discovering the beauty of prayer. The leader (the one with the same DNA as Steve Jobs!) became very solemn and in a calm but serious voice said, "Sir... you don't have to worry. These planes fly from here to Houston every day... and they *never* crash!"

"Today, as the Church seeks to experience a profound missionary renewal, there is a kind of preaching which falls to each of us as a daily responsibility. It has to do with bringing the Gospel to the people we meet, whether they be our neighbors or complete strangers. This is the informal preaching which takes place in the middle of a conversation, something along the lines of what a missionary does when visiting a home. Being a disciple means being constantly ready to bring the love of Jesus to others, and this can happen unexpectedly and in any place: on the street, in a city square, during work, on a journey."

"In this preaching, which is always respectful and gentle, the first step is always personal dialogue, when the other person shares his or her joys, hopes and concerns for loved ones, or so many other heartfelt needs." (EG, 127-128)

Back in Robstown, Texas, with Christmas fast approaching, everyone at the SOLT Motherhouse (Casa San Jose) was making plans regarding what they should do for Christmas. Fr. Flanagan suggested to the few seminarians present that they should consider visiting our orphanage in central Mexico. I was eager to follow up on Fr. Jim's idea so I asked the other 2 seminarians if they would like to go. Unfortunately, they had different plans... which left me in something of a quandary. I wasn't sure if I wanted to make an overnight bus excursion to Queretaro by myself. It's always nice, and generally recommended, to have a companion on such trips.

I came to the conclusion that if the Founder suggested it, then it was a legitimate mission and the Lord would certainly be with me. I took a small backpack with personal items, and a little duffle bag filled with colorful rosaries for the children. The thing I didn't have much of was money. I managed to scrape together just enough money for a round-trip bus ticket. Someone gave me a lift to the border, then I crossed the international bridge into Nuevo Laredo, MX, and made my way to the bus station.

When I arrived at the bus station I was shocked to see how busy and congested it was... there were cars and people everywhere!

I could barely get in the door, but once inside I realized what was going on. When it comes to travel, Americans are "airplane people"... Mexicans, however, are "bus people". I had forgotten this and was beginning to feel a bit uneasy. I got on a long line to buy a ticket, but before I even reached the counter a man announced that all the buses to Queretaro were full and there would be no more until the following day.

I went out to the sidewalk and did some quick thinking. "Maybe I could take a plane?" I thought. But with so little money I would never have enough to get there... never mind the return trip! I don't really know how to explain it, but something told me to just go... that somehow I would make it to the orphanage. I hailed a cab... "El aeropuerto, por favor." I was planning to check the fares when I got to the airport... maybe I would get lucky! If not, I would still have enough money to get back to the border.

The Nuevo Laredo airport was relatively quiet and it didn't take long to find out that my original sense of what the fares would be was correct... I had just barely enough money to buy a one-way ticket to Monterrey (a big city in northern Mexico that is a little closer, but still very far from my final destination). Now, I really had a decision to make; should I continue... or should I turn back? What would I do when I arrived in Monterrey penniless? I had no idea. But something just kept telling me to stay calm and keep moving forward... one step at a time. I bought a ticket, boarded the plane, and had to laugh at myself. "What are you doing? This is totally crazy! This would be a bad idea in the USA, but in Mexico... where I don't know anyone and have less than kindergarten level Spanish... this is incredibly reckless!"

"The Church which 'goes forth' is a community of missionary disciples who take the first step, who are involved and supportive, who bear fruit and rejoice. An evangelizing community knows that the Lord has taken the initiative, he has loved us first, and therefore we can move forward, boldly take the initiative, go out to others, seek those who have fallen away, stand at the crossroads and welcome the out-cast. Let us try

a little harder to take the first step and to become involved." (EG, 24)

The airport in Monterrey is a super busy place they call a "hub" because so many flights leave from there. After asking around, however, I discovered there were no flights to Queretaro. My final destination was a quaint little town named Colon just outside of Queretaro in the foothills that lead up to the high sierra. I was told that Queretaro was about a 2-hour drive from San Luis Potosi and there was a flight, a small commuter plane, going to San Luis in less than an hour. I decided my best bet was to get on that small plane. Easier said than done! What was I going to do... offer to wash dishes like a person might do if he or she couldn't pay their restaurant bill?

I leaned up against a big pillar in the middle of that bustling airport with people coming and going directly in front of me, and I asked the Lord to guide me. All of a sudden, in the midst of this sea of humanity I spotted 2 older men who were speaking English. I approached them and asked if they knew anything about the little 29 passenger plane that goes to San Luis. They said they never used it, but the airline it belonged to had an excellent reputation. I found out they were college instructors heading back to the states. They asked about me, and I told them my story and how my only hope for getting to the orphanage was to take the flight to San Luis. I showed them the beautiful rosaries that were to be a surprise Christmas gift for the children. I then explained that if they could help me get to the orphanage I would ask the children to pray for them using their new rosaries!

I don't know where the words came from, but only someone with a heart of stone could have said "no" to that pitch. As providence would have it, the professors were truly compassionate individuals. Ticket in hand, I went over to the boarding area to wait for my flight to be called. I still didn't know what I was going to do when I arrived in San Luis Potosi. Time was moving on, and the plane was scheduled to land in San Luis around 5pm. I wasn't comfortable with the idea of being in a strange city with darkness approaching and no money in my pocket. Perhaps I could seek refuge in a nearby parish? Then again, maybe not... I tried that once when my car broke down in the states and the pastor told me he didn't believe me and if I phoned again or showed up at his rectory he would call the police.

The plane wasn't due to take off for ½ an hour, so I started looking around at the gate to see if there were any English speaking passengers on the flight who I could chat with while waiting. I spotted 2 young men who appeared to be just about the same age as me, so I went over and introduced myself asking if they were also going to San Luis. They said they were, so we began to converse and share information about ourselves. They said they were from Texas and were involved in telecommunications. I told them I was a missionary on my way to visit an orphanage.

As the conversation developed and they heard how the Lord was providing for me, and that I had no idea what I would do when I arrived in San Luis, they were captivated. "Larry... this is an incredible story!" one of them exclaimed, "Listen... why don't you come with us. We're going to San Miguel de Allende... my family owns a vacation home there. My girlfriend will be picking us up, and it's about a 2 hour drive to San Miguel. Also, Larry... something you probably don't know. Colon... the little town you're going to... is just over on the other side of the mountains from San Miguel!"

We were about 15 minutes out from San Miguel when the fellow whose family owned the home we were going to called the house to let them know we were getting close and that I was with them. His mother told him some cousins had shown up unexpectedly and there simply was no room for another guest. It would seem my streak of providential interventions was coming to an end. Not at all... in fact, they were about to get better! His mother instructed him to get me a room in the best hotel in San Miguel and take me to dinner at the finest restaurant!

After dinner I was told that someone would come to my hotel in the morning and lead me to the restaurant where the entire family would be meeting for breakfast. He said his mother and the rest of his relatives were anxious to meet me and to learn more about my mission adventure. Then, he continued, after breakfast they would pay a taxi to take me to the orphanage… but only after giving me a proper tour of beautiful San Miguel. What a magnificent family! And the Lord knew all along that in his providence he was going to lead me to them. All I had to do was trust him.

The orphanage was all decked out for Christmas and everyone was in a festive, holiday spirit. The children loved their rosaries and were very moved by the story of how the Lord himself made sure the rosaries were delivered to them safely. And that's really the point here; God will not be outdone in charity. If a person begins to move in God's love, the Spirit will take over. I was beginning to understand Fr. John's teaching about how the missionary must "live in the Spirit."

"We become fully human when we become more than human, when we let God bring us beyond ourselves in order to attain the fullest truth of our being. Here we find the source and inspiration of all our efforts at evangelization. For if we have received the love which restores meaning to our lives, how can we fail to share that love with others?" (EG, 8)

Fr. Lawrence Edward Tucker, SOLT

Chapter Four

LIVING IN THE SPIRIT

The day before my ordination to the priesthood, my superior asked me where I would like to serve for my first assignment. He said to list three choices by order of preference, but all 3 should be in Latin America. Belize was my first choice, the orphanage was second, and Nuevo Laredo, MX, was last. In the morning I was told my assignment would be Nuevo Laredo. Although it was not my first choice, the assignment made sense because I had been visiting Nuevo Laredo for years and already had a number of contacts there.

I asked my superior if he thought there was anyone who might like to join me as part of my team. He responded with a very telling but honest, "No". To understand this rather unusual response, one need only make a little visit to *Las Nuevas Colonias* of Nuevo Laredo, Mexico. Upon seeing what looks like an immense, dirt-poor refugee camp, you would know immediately why very few people want to go there. Three months of the year the temperature is in the high nineties, and in June, July, and August the mercury is usually between 100 and 115°F. I remember a couple of days one summer when it was hotter in Nuevo Laredo than it was in Death Valley! At night, if the temperature drops below 98.6°F (body temperature), you might be able to get some sleep… if you have a fan. But if the night time temperature is above 100°F, even with a fan chances are you will feel nauseous and will not be able to sleep.

Putting aside the difficult realities of a harsh desert climate, the *barrio* (neighborhood) itself is so overcrowded and impoverished one could easily write it off as a hopeless case. Spread across the low rolling hills as far as the eye can see, like an illusion that floats in and out of the heat vapors, is a sea of hovels... one more unworthy of human habitation than the other. Most of these humble dwellings are composed of materials that have fallen off trucks... or that the people find at places where such things are dumped when considered no longer useful. "Building materials" such as damaged wooden pallets, rusty pieces of corrugated tin, broken sections of waterlogged plywood, battered and torn plastic tarps, and any other material that could be used in constructing a primitive shelter are collected and used in a truly creative way. Nevertheless, backyard sheds in the USA are better constructed than the ramshackle huts that litter this bone-dry, treeless landscape.

I asked my superior if he would mind if I did my own recruiting since he could not think of anyone willing to join the new mission. He was fine with the idea as long as the person I found was not already assigned. I stepped out of his office and began walking down the main hallway en-route to the chapel. As I was straining to think of who I could possibly approach and ask to join my team, little did I know the person God had already chosen just exited the chapel and was approaching me!

"Hello Br. Michael", I said... sensing that he could be a likely candidate for this unpopular mission, "Do you have a few minutes... I'd like to talk with you about something." We went into the living room and I began my sales-pitch thusly... "Brother, are you assigned anywhere?" "No... not yet", he responded. "Great... I'm glad to hear that. Brother... I'm being sent to Mexico to build a maternity clinic and a feeding center for children, and I'd like to have you on my team."

Brother was around 63 years old at the time and was in such poor health that some people thought he should be in a nursing home. He was legally blind, had epilepsy, and was born with a genetic disorder called Osler-Weber-Rendu Syndrome (you might think that someone with this kind of medical history would be bitter and difficult to get along with; that was not the case... he had a stable and consistently cheerful personality). Osler-Weber patients have genetically malformed capillaries that break and cause bleeding in various parts of the body. With Brother Michael, the problem was primarily located in his sinuses. Brother's mother had the problem in a more insidious location... the intestines. One day, in the kitchen of his home, she fell down dead right in front of him. She was only 54 years old. Brother himself would not have lived as long as he did were it not for the development of *Laser Cauterization*.

"Where in Mexico are you going?" questioned the good brother. Br. Michael knew Mexico quite well and liked it very much. He was fluent in English, Spanish, and Latin; and had a working knowledge of German, Italian, Polish, and Yiddish... not to mention a complete mastery of English and Spanish grammar. "A Mexican border town called Nuevo Laredo, Brother. It's two hours from here just across the river from Laredo, TX. Our mission is on the perimeter of the city in a section called Las Nuevas Colonias. Have you ever been there?" The answer to this question was critical. If he had been there chances were he would make some excuse as to why he couldn't go. "I've been to Nuevo Laredo... but I've never been to Las Nuevas Colonias. What's it like there?"

OK... now the ball's in my court. I could "candy coat" my description of Las Nuevas Colonias, but when he saw what they were really like he would never trust me again. I chose to do the exact opposite. "Brother... I'm going to describe for you what it's like there. Imagine this town where we are right now a few days after a nuclear holocaust. That's what the colonias are like. It's a wretched place Bro... wicked hot with a whole lot of human misery in the midst of such extreme poverty it will leave you speechless."

"Sure... sign me up... I love Mexico!" was his immediate response. *"Viva La Virgen de Guadalupe!"* I thought to myself. Before he came to SOLT, Brother was in a new community called *The Brothers of Our Lady of Guadalupe*. In fact, he helped Bishop Jerome Hastrich of the missionary diocese of Gallup, New Mexico, found the new community. Br. Michael was the first superior and the first Novice Master. He was also the Bishop's assistant for 25 years. As icing on the cake, not only did brother have an abundance of Church experience… he had a memory like a steel trap. Whereas most people have a hard time remembering things, Brother had a hard time forgetting them! If he saw something, heard something, or read something… he would never forget it.

"Now, Fr. Larry", Brother began, "you realize… there's not much I can do to help you." Because of brother's genetic situation he would bleed from the nose profusely around 7 times a day. These episodes would leave him in a weakened condition for around 20 minutes. Any kind of stress or tension would only make the hemorrhaging worse. It could happen anywhere at any time. As a side-effect of this rare condition, Brother had perfect posture. For his entire life he walked with his head back and his face tilted upward so that when the capillaries in his sinus cavities burst, due to the position of his head he would have an additional split second to whip out his hanky and catch the blood flowing down his chin and neck before it hit his clothes.

At 5'8" and 175lb's, with perfect posture, white hair parted on the side, eyeglasses, and perfect usage and enunciation of the English language… Brother made a rather distinguished appearance. But with his face aimed skyward and his vision compromised, Brother was an accident waiting to happen. Because his line of sight was raised, he was always tripping over things on the ground he didn't see. Occasionally, in the blink of an eye, he would go right to the ground like a tree felled by a lumberjack; one second he was there… the next, he was gone!

Given his professorial appearance, these sanguineous episodes were all the more incongruous and bordering on the absurd. At first, I was startled by these sudden Osler-Weber events. But after a while I barely noticed them. Once we were having an "early-bird-special" dinner at a restaurant in San Antonio, TX, when Brother's genetically flawed capillaries decided to act up. Without any warning, blood gushed out all over the white linen tablecloth. It must have looked like a mafia hit or something because the women in the restaurant jumped up from their chairs and began screaming. I, on the other hand, was as calm as could be and continued to slice my chicken parmesan, barely even noticing the gory scene that was taking place only inches away from me. I knew that Brother had everything under control and in a minute or two the bleeding would stop and he would be back to normal.

Well, as the saying goes, "one man's ceiling is another man's floor". The people in the restaurant were not desensitized to Br. Michael's condition, and I'm quite sure they knew nothing about Osler-Weber-Rendu Syndrome (there are many physicians who have never heard of it). Finally, the screaming stopped, but the people were now trying to get out of the restaurant. The restaurant staff came over to our table, lifted Brother up and laid him on a cushioned bench against the wall. At this point, I put down my fork and tried to explain to them that Brother was fine... that this goes on all day, every day. Because of my seemingly disinterested attitude towards a man who appeared to be bleeding to death, I had the distinct feeling that the restaurant staff suspected I might be responsible for Brother's "injury"! They were just about to call an ambulance (and perhaps the police!) when Brother himself finally convinced them that he was OK and this gruesome event was nothing unusual for him.

When Brother confessed that there was very little he could do in a mission, I wanted to put him at ease. "Brother... I haven't asked you to help because of what you can do. I've asked you to join my team because of *who* you are! You are Br. Michael *of The Precious Blood* (Fr. Flanagan gave him this name when he joined SOLT). Your sufferings and sacrifices will bring countless blessings to the mission. Besides, Brother... you're going to be the brains of the operation. You've got the experience and knowledge I lack."

"Where are we going to live, Fr. Larry... have you figured that one out yet?" Brother asked with a very interested look on his face. "I put the word out on the street that we need a place in Nuevo Laredo so we can work with the poor in Las Nuevas Colonias", I said, "I'm sure someone will offer us a little house to use." I had placed a notice on the bulletin board of an enormous Adoration Chapel in Nuevo Laredo. In the notice, I mentioned that we could not afford to pay rent but we would fix the house up and maintain it.

If we were members of one of the wealthy orders in the Church we would have just purchased a piece of property in the Colonias and built a suitable religious house. But we are not an affluent community. Quite the opposite in fact... we are a very poor community. Our founder had insight into something Pope Francis has been speaking about that many are hearing for the first time. Francis said, *"I want a Church which is poor and for the poor"* (EG: 198). Being a poor community creates a completely different context for doing missionary work. We rely on God for "our daily bread", as it were. This precarious way of being in the world... this humiliation... facilitates our sensitivity to the poor and our preaching of the Gospel.

Brother seemed satisfied with this plan regarding a house and, sure enough, someone called asking us to come to Nuevo Laredo to check out a house they wanted to offer us. I asked the caller where the house was, hoping that it was either in the colonias or at least close to them. Their answer left me somewhat disappointed. The house was near the Cathedral, they said... in Colonia Longoria. Well, not only is Colonia Longoria quite a distance from our mission, it's also the wealthiest colonia in the city! I probably should have told the benefactor immediately that a residence in that part of the city would be out of the question, but I've learned from experience it's always good to at least meet those individuals who offer to help with God's work.

When we arrived at the address the benefactor gave us, we burst out laughing. It was the famous old Longoria Mansion... the biggest house in the city! It was prominently located right at the head of the Plaza, facing the Cathedral (The Longoria family built the Cathedral as well as the mansion, but they no longer owned the mansion). Talk about stunned! You may have heard the expression... *This does not compute.* If it ever applied anywhere, it definitely applied here. The Longoria Mansion was more or less a replica, although smaller, of 1600 Pennsylvania Ave... the White House! We composed ourselves, got out of the car and followed the benefactor into the house... I mean, mansion.

She took us through the kitchen and into the formal dining room. The dining room table was so long, if you were sitting at the head and wanted to communicate with someone at the other end you would probably have to use a megaphone! And the chandelier suspended over the center of the table was so massive and glitzy it reminded me of pictures I'd seen of futuristic space stations. The benefactor turned to me and asked a question that struck me as so thoroughly ludicrous it was all I could do to keep from laughing. "Do you think this will be suitable, Fr. Larry?" I was very tempted to say, "No... the table is much too small and the chandelier insufficient... hardly worth using!"

Of course I would never say such a thing... not even in jest. What I did say was, "More than suitable... MUCH more than suitable!" As she continued to give us a tour of the various rooms of the mansion I was trying to figure out why we were being offered such an inappropriate residence. Did she think we were looking for a general headquarters for our community? "Let's take the elevator downstairs," she said, "I want to show you the discotheque." I looked at Br. Michael and whispered, "elevator? discotheque?"

The Disco was very nice… the theme was Africa; everything was covered with Zebra and Leopard print materials. "You could have very nice parties here, Father!" the benefactor said. Parties? Sure… everyone knows that missionaries are card-carrying party animals! Forget about parties… that Disco was big enough for a world class *Rave*! Was this really happening? Were we really missionaries scoping out the Disco in a mansion being offered to serve as our residence while we worked with the poor?

"What's going on here?" I thought, "Something is wrong with this picture." The benefactor took us back to the main floor and down the hall to the luxuriously wide, marble, winding staircase that led to the 2nd floor. Not far from where the stairs began was a beautiful Grand Piano. Brother Michael, an accomplished pianist who gave recitals in his youth, spotted it immediately and threw me a look as if to say, "Let's not rule this place out too quickly." I immediately threw a look back at him which said, "Brother… let's keep it real!"

The landing at the second floor had a back wall of solid glass from ceiling to floor that looked out upon a magnificent backyard… complete with an extremely large swimming pool and a couple of tennis courts. Because of my love for swimming, I was just about to give Br. Michael the same look he had just given me regarding the Grand Piano… but somehow I managed to stay focused. Our tour guide told us that on Sunday afternoons the Bishop and his canon lawyer played tennis on one of the courts.

"Sure," I thought, "I can picture it now." One fine Sunday afternoon the Bishop rings the front doorbell and I answer the door. "Fr. Larry! What are you doing here?" "Actually, Bishop… I live here now." "Is that Br. Michael over there playing the Grand Piano?" asks

the stunned Bishop. "The one and only! He's just brushing up on his
Rachmaninoff. Is there something I can help you with, Bishop?"
"Well, eh, yes… we normally use one of the tennis courts on Sunday
afternoons." Then I would respond, "Yes… so I've heard.
Unfortunately, Bishop… those days are over. This is a religious
house now and we like to maintain an atmosphere of recollection.
Sorry… will you excuse me? It's time for my daily swim… good
day."

This was just one of the comical scenarios Brother and I
dreamed up as we crossed the international bridge back into Texas.
We told our benefactor in the most gracious way possible that
although it was beautiful, it was much more house than we needed
and we would never be able to pay the electric bill… never mind all
the other expenses such a place would require. We never did find out
why the mansion was unoccupied and being offered to us.
Sometimes, I think the Lord used this incident to show us how easy
it is for him to provide everything and anything we need, but the
greatest gift he could ever bestow upon us was the privilege of
serving his beloved poor.

*"This practical relativism consists in acting as if God did not exist, making
decisions as if the poor did not exist, setting goals as if others did not exist, working as if
people who have not received the Gospel did not exist. It is striking that even some who
clearly have solid doctrinal and spiritual convictions frequently fall into a lifestyle which
leads to an attachment to financial security, or to a desire for power or human glory at all
cost, rather than giving their lives to others in mission. Let us not allow ourselves to be
robbed of missionary enthusiasm!" (EG, 80)*

After we were offered an appropriate house to use and
finally settled in… the real challenge began. It's not easy for an
American to construct a building in Mexico. The "red tape" involved
is very red… and very long. Everyone wants "a piece of the
action"… that is; everyone wants your US dollars. Apart from
building the clinic, we also had pastoral responsibility for a mission
chapel in the colonias. Despite the deep faith and heartfelt generosity

of our people, the Sunday collection in the chapel was not even enough to gas-up the truck. But the Lord provided for our work with the poor by giving me a daily Mass at a well-known convent across the river in Laredo, TX.

For those who have never crossed the international bridge that passes over the Rio Grande connecting Nuevo Laredo, MX, and Laredo, TX, you might imagine it to be a simple matter. It isn't. On a good day, it will take around ½ an hour. On a really bad day, say around Christmas, it could take 4 hours or more. Normally, it takes about an hour to cross. As you leave Mexico, you have to pay a toll. This causes an enormous bumper-to-bumper traffic jam for around 6 or 7 blocks. After the toll there is another traffic nightmare because each vehicle must stop on the USA side of the bridge at a review area where a license plate check is done. Then, the driver will have to answer certain questions and produce a valid ID before entering the USA.

I was pulled aside once by the customs officials for a thorough inspection of my truck. I watched nervously as they went through my vehicle with a fine tooth comb (I had heard stories of traffickers hiding drugs in vehicles that crossed daily and always went to the same destination). When they opened my Mass kit and saw my vestments, hosts, chalice, missal, etc… they nodded their heads as if to say: "He's for real". They apologized and said: "Father… we stopped you because last week a drug trafficker disguised as a priest tried to get through here, but we caught him."

Brother Michael and I went through this ordeal every day, 7 days a week, for 2 years. We started to think of the bridge as our "home away from home". The desperately poor people of Nuevo Laredo were also very aware of the terrible traffic situation at the entrance to the bridge, but to them it wasn't terrible… it was a golden opportunity; a captive group of prospective donors right on their doorstep! Thanks to the bridge there was no need to wander the streets of the city begging. They could stand in one spot in the midst of the traffic jam and petition each driver for a *limosna* (offering) as the cars filed past ever so slowly.

In time, we came to know all of the poor people by name. Their situations covered a spectrum that went from bad… to worse… to off the chart! A desperately poor, skin and bones indigenous woman with a mal-nourished baby in her arms was *bad*. A blind man missing a hand was *worse*. An elderly, blind woman missing an arm and a leg was *off the chart*! Most of the poor people, however, were not afflicted with any visible handicap but struggled with hunger, lived on the streets, and were very poorly dressed.

When this little tribe of desperados spotted our vehicle they would rush over and congregate at the driver's window, form a line and ask for a blessing. Amazingly, very few asked for money. Such is the faith of the poor! I gave them rosaries, miraculous medals, and occasionally small, paperback New Testaments in Spanish. But the main thing we did was to listen to their stories… their hopes, their fears, their sufferings. This daily gathering at my car of around 10 to 20 poor people became so routine and so Spirit-filled, I decided to give it a name. I called it our *Bridge Ministry*.

One day, we arrived at the street that leads up to the bridge… *Avenida Santos Degollados* (Santos Degollados means "the beheaded saints"; but the avenue was probably named after a famous Mexican General named Santos Degollados). As we expected, it was backed up for many blocks. Just as we had done hundreds of times before, we eased into the slow parade of cars that were so close together they seemed more like a train. As soon as our "parishioners" spotted us they rushed over to greet us. We always drove in the left lane close to the sidewalk so they could line up safely.

As we crept along, stop-and-go… all the while ministering to a most uncommon assortment of desperate human beings, it must have looked like a group of street actors reenacting a scene from *Les Misérables*. Nothing unusual about that… things were going along as abnormally as they normally did. All of a sudden, I heard loud shouting in Spanish. I looked in my rear view mirror and saw that the driver of the pickup truck directly behind me, a middle-aged Hispanic man, was screaming at me.

St. John the Evangelist said that God is Love. Sometimes, if a person is angry with God, they may find expressions of love hard to bear. I suspect the driver behind us fell into that category. He was demanding that we stop ministering to the poor. Apparently, our loving service to people excluded and rejected by society was driving the man crazy. He was cursing and threatening to harm me if I continued to manifest our Father's mercy to his little children. If any of the poor were absent-minded enough to venture over towards the incensed driver, he would practically leap out the window of his truck, cursing and flailing his arms. I would have understood someone being upset if our work with the poor was holding up traffic… but that was not at all the case.

The first message our irate neighbor sent me, via the universal language of hand gestures, was the slamming of his fisted right hand into his open left hand… repeatedly. "Ok, I get it… you don't like me helping the poor and you'd like to punch me in the face," I thought to myself, "Sorry… but their serious need comes before your petty likes and dislikes. *'Get thee to'*… an Anger Management workshop!"

The next "endearing" message he sent was another well-known classic… the one where the person wraps their hands around their throat to signal they are going to strangle you. A little further along, his anger escalating with each new person I dealt with, he pulled yet another threatening gesture out of his quiver of sick, hateful signs. This time he put his first two fingers up against his throat as if it were a blade, then he ran the "blade" across his throat and around his entire neck as if to say: "I'm going to cut your head off!"

OK... forget about Anger Management... we're way beyond that. With this last message, we're talking homicidal maniac! I couldn't help but think... how strange that we should be threatened with decapitation on a street named after The Beheaded Saints. I turned to Brother and told him what I had just seen in my rear view mirror and asked him if I should stop ministering to the poor. "NO!" he said, "Absolutely not. Continue to serve them."

I told Brother to be prepared for anything. There was one block to go before the toll and just a few more "parishioners" to talk with. I felt certain our enraged friend would, at the very least, jump out of his truck and smash our rear window with a tire iron. Brother Michael didn't seem to be the least bit concerned. I could imagine the maniacal driver showing up at Brother's window breathing hate and venom... and Brother correcting the fool's Spanish grammar!

Precisely at the midpoint of the bridge, there is a white line around a foot wide painted on the roadway. That white line is the border. On one side is Mexico... on the other, the USA. Occasionally, a poor person is able to sneak past the toll guards and with great stealth work their way through the log-jam of slow moving cars until they reach the white line. Once there, they stand on the Mexico side of the line and, free from all competition, work the cars as they creep by. I think the idea is that the drivers feel a sense of relief knowing they are just inches away from the USA and this improved frame of mind will work in the poor person's favor (being poor does not mean being unintelligent!).

As we approached the middle of the bridge we could see someone standing there holding out a cup for donations. We had met the individual before, but we didn't know him that well. He was a sorry sight; a young man around 18 years old with only one arm, one eye, and a deformed leg. When we reached him, he recognized me and asked for a blessing. I reached out of the car window, put my hands on his head and blessed him. I also warned him about the driver behind us… how he might not be his best "customer" of the day.

I don't know who invented the rear view mirror but whoever it was deserves a round of applause because what I saw in it that day was just astonishing! As we pulled away from the young man and rolled over the line into the USA, my eyes were glued to the rear view mirror. I was trying to monitor our deranged stalker to see how he would deal with the innocent soul I just blessed. When the unhinged driver reached the poor youth, I couldn't believe what I saw. I told Brother Michael to turn around immediately so he could witness a miracle. The same man who just minutes before was so infuriated he would have been a perfect candidate for a straitjacket, was now throwing handfuls of money not just at his cup but all over the jubilant youth! When he was done showering the lad with US currency (bills!), the driver, who was now as gentle as a lamb, made eye contact with me via my rear view mirror. Then, with tears rolling down his face, he made the sign of the cross and gave me a salute. I held up my right hand so he could see it and gave him a blessing.

How mysterious and wonderful are the ways of God! What were the chances that an individual such as the one we encountered would find himself trapped directly behind missionaries who for 40 minutes did nothing other than serve the outcasts of society? Apparently, the Lord knew that witnessing God's love in action was exactly what that man needed.

"I prefer a Church which is bruised, hurting and dirty because it has been out on the streets, rather than a Church which is unhealthy from being confined and clinging to its own security. I do not want a Church concerned with being at the center and then ends by being caught up in a web of obsessions and procedures. More than by fear of going astray, my hope is that we will be moved by the fear of remaining shut up within structures which give us a false sense of security, within rules which make us harsh judges,

within habits which make us feel safe, while at our door people are starving and Jesus does not tire of saying to us: 'Give them something to eat' (Mk 6:37)." (EG, 49)

Fr. Lawrence Edward Tucker, SOLT

Chapter Five

SERVING WITH JOY

Sometimes between assignments, missionaries will reside at the Motherhouse of their community until everything is in order for the new assignment. It could be that the missionary is waiting for a visa to clear… or perhaps it's a question of going through a long, drawn out application process for a grant that is critical to the new mission. Whatever the reason, these lay-overs at the community's Administrative Headquarters are generally refreshing and enjoyable… a welcome opportunity to reconnect with other members of the community.

I was enjoying one of these intermissions at our Motherhouse when I was asked to help in a parish our community staffs on the other side of town. There was a big community gathering taking place in another part of the country and all our priests, including the pastor of St. Anthony's, wanted to attend. Fr. Bob and I, being the "greenhorns" in town with only 2 years of priestly experience, were given the task of staying behind and watching over St. Anthony's parish. The assignment would only be from a Monday to a Friday… at which time all the priests and administrators were due back.

St. Anthony's is a Mexican-American parish in a fairly large South Texas town named Robstown. When the Bishop of Corpus Christi, TX, invited our community to set up our General Headquarters in his diocese he gave us St. Anthony's as our primary apostolate. Most of the people in Robstown are Church-going Catholics… which makes St. Anthony's one of the bigger parishes in the diocese. The parish has a large rectory, convent, adoration chapel, elementary school, and a social service center.

Fr. Bob and I were old friends and both of us had a great love for the Mexican people and their culture. We were excited and looking forward to being the resident shepherds of this beautiful flock of God's people. Of course, we knew that it would be relatively quiet considering that the Church had been closed down for renovations and the schedule had been modified accordingly. Little did we know that God had his own plans for the parish that week and things were about to shift into high gear.

Monday went very well. The parish was tranquil and everything unfolded smoothly and without incident. That evening after dinner, we reflected on how we had been somewhat apprehensive regarding our new responsibilities. But now that one full day was drawing to a close and the parish was still in one piece, we could breathe a sigh of relief. It appeared we were in fact up to the task and would almost certainly make it through the week. We knew from stories we had heard, as well as from our own experience, that, given the right priest (or I should say, the wrong priest!), a parish could practically be dismantled in the course of one weekend.

The neighborhood immediately surrounding the parish property is rich with traditional Mexican culture. Some of the families even own chickens… and the roosters can be counted on to faithfully announce the dawning of each new day. Tuesday was no different. It was ushered in by the roosters, along with Brother Sun, and proceeded in such profound peace that it seemed as if time had melted into eternity. We had no way of knowing that this was just the calm before the storm.

After lunch, I told Fr. Bob I was going upstairs to my room for a siesta. He said he would be in his office catching up on some work. About an hour later, I heard a knock on my door. "Fr. Larry… it's Fr. Bob." "I'll be downstairs in around half an hour", I yelled…

more asleep than awake. "It's important, Fr. Larry... I need to talk with you." "What's so important?" I said in a somewhat irritated voice. "Fr. Larry... look out your window."

I rolled out of bed and stumbled over to the window with the blanket still wrapped around me. I looked down at the little street that separates the elementary school from the rectory and the Church. I couldn't believe what I saw. I literally had to rub the sleep from my eyes and look around the room to make sure I was still in St. Anthony's rectory. The normally quiet (actually, quiet is not the right word; *dead* is the right word!)... the normally dead little street was now as crowded and chaotic as Fifth Avenue in Manhattan, New York City, at the high point of the Easter Parade! There were police cars and policemen everywhere... except in those places where there were TV station trucks, reporters, and camera crews! Winding in and out of this three ring circus of police and media hyper activity was a very long line of people protected by police barricades. I could see that this mysterious grouping of people extended into the main entrance of the Church... at which point my visual contact ended.

I ran over to the door, threw it open... and there stood Fr. Bob with a big grin on his face. "What's going on?" I said in a state of total confusion. "Sit down, Fr. Larry, and I'll bring you up to speed. While you were resting something amazing happened. One of the workers in the Church pulled up the carpeting in the spot where the Tabernacle had been. As he pulled up the carpeting, he noticed something on the plywood flooring that immediately caught his attention. There before him was a beautiful image of Our Lady of Guadalupe!"

Fr. Bob went on to say that the man was practically speechless with wonder as he looked upon this marvelous sight. He called the other workers to come and see what he had discovered. They were all filled with awe as they gazed at the lovely image of their mother. The worker who made the discovery ran into the rectory to report the phenomenon to the secretary, who immediately told Fr. Bob. By the time Fr. Bob got over to the Church to take a look at the reported discovery, there was already a line of people forming to see it. Word got out very quickly because there had been some people praying in the back of the Church. Something of this nature would be very well received by the humble, faith-filled people of Robstown, and they would waste no time in responding to such an occurrence. They would see it as a golden opportunity to manifest the love and devotion they have for their heavenly mother... *La Virgencita de Guadalupe.*

The police and various TV News stations must have been contacted immediately because they were on the scene very shortly after the discovery. When Fr. Bob came back from the Church after having seen the image for the first time, he discussed it with the secretary who had also just finished viewing the image. The image was about 3 feet in length, and although it was not perfect, it was clear enough to recognize the essential figure of Our Lady of Guadalupe. Both Fr. Bob and the secretary were deeply moved by it.

Having been duly informed so that Fr. Bob and I were now on the same page regarding this incredible turn of events, we went downstairs into Fr. Bob's office and just sat there staring at one another. After a minute or so, each of us smiled and began to express our amazement. What else could we do? Both of us knew that because of this event we would be in for an extremely challenging week... the direct opposite of what we were expecting. Nevertheless, we were so filled with joy we could barely contain ourselves! Half joking, I said, "Fr. Bob... you're in charge; what should we do?" Fr. Bob looked at me with a big question mark on his face. "I'm in charge? Who said that I'm in charge? I think you're in charge!" It was then that we realized the question of who would be in charge had never been clearly addressed.

Using an inconspicuous entrance, we decided to sneak into

the Church so I could view the image for the first time. We managed to avoid being detected by the reporters who had been looking for us, and I worked my way through the crowd surrounding the image. As I looked down at the image I too was moved by its simple beauty. But the thing that impressed me more was the profound reverence of the people as they gazed upon their mother with deep, heartfelt love and gratitude. Nothing like this had ever happened before in Robstown and the people felt greatly honored at having been chosen for such a special blessing.

"Closer to our own time, Benedict XVI, speaking about Latin America, pointed out that popular piety is 'a precious treasure of the Catholic Church', in which 'we see the soul of the Latin American peoples'." (EG, 123)

On the way back to the Church we were intercepted by a clever reporter who figured out our not so secret route. He got hold of Fr. Bob, and I continued on to the rectory. The main thing the reporter wanted to know was whether or not the image was supernatural. We didn't spend 4 years in the seminary for nothing... we both knew the answer to that question, but it might not be what the reporter wanted to hear. Fr. Bob told him the simple truth; only the Bishop could determine whether or not the image was supernatural.

When Fr. Bob arrived back inside the rectory we both agreed he had handled the reporter well and that if we kept this up we might survive this thing after all. It was about 6pm, and it was time to get down to business... we really needed a plan. The first and the biggest question we faced was should we allow the people to continue to reverence the image? The line was getting longer and longer and there was always the possibility that someone would say it was some sort of a hoax. The whole thing could backfire. As we discussed this question we realized there was another issue of possibly greater urgency: the interior of the Church was a construction site and there were hazards all over the place; bricks, stones, tiles, wire, glass, cement, paint, and tools scattered in every direction. For this reason, the finding of the image took on the character of a discovery made at an archeological dig!

We didn't realize it at the time but these two decisions were critical and would determine the success or failure of everything that was to follow. As we discussed the first question regarding the viewing of the image, we quickly realized that it would simply be inhuman and heartless to prevent these beautiful, humble people from expressing their deeply felt religious sentiments. After all, it was their parish… and *La Virgencita de Guadalupe* was their mother! We thought that the whole thing would probably die down in a few days and everything would be back to normal by the time our superiors returned.

"The Aparecida Document describes the riches which the Holy Spirit pours forth in popular piety by his gratuitous initiative. It is 'a legitimate way of living the faith'… it brings with itself the grace of being a missionary, of coming out of oneself and setting out on pilgrimage: 'Journeying together to shrines and taking part in other manifestations of popular piety… is in itself an evangelizing gesture.' Let us not stifle or presume to control this missionary power!" (EG, 124)

The next issue to be resolved was the one concerning the dangerous condition of the Church interior. If we were to continue with the viewing, we would have to move the image to a safe location. This would also be necessary so that the workers could finish the refurbishing of the Church on schedule. We considered a few possibilities, but the one that made the most sense was the sacristy. It was connected to the Church, was just about the right size, and had a private entrance. Very conveniently, it had an alcove in the back where the image could be displayed, and an island in the middle which would be perfect for directing the flow of traffic in and out of the sacristy.

Fr. Bob and I agreed that the sacristy was "born" for this mission, and we directed the construction crew to cut the image out of the plywood in the form of a rectangle... as though it was going to be put in a frame. We asked the people to leave the Church so we could work on the image, but they were welcome to return in the morning to reverence the image in its new home... the sacristy. The people were very docile and compliant and everything regarding the extraction and relocation of the image went just as planned. It was Tuesday evening, and we returned to the rectory for a light dinner and to work up a plan for the next few days.

A happening such as this is so rare that there are very few people around who can describe how it feels to be caught up in such a unique spiritual event. Although words fall short, the best I can do is to say that the flow of joy into the soul is so abundant that one could easily lose track of time and everything associated with it... for example: eating, sleeping, etc. The person is so elevated by a type of holy mirth that it seems as if one has somehow made contact with heaven itself! When Fr. Bob and I would pass one another in a hallway, we would look at each other and just start laughing! It's good there was no one else in the house because they would have thought both of us were inebriated. The whole thing was so disorienting we hardly knew if we were in Robstown, TX... or Lourdes, France!

"Our Christian joy drinks of his brimming heart. Wherever the disciples went, 'there was great joy' (Jn 8:8); even amid persecution they continued to be 'filled with joy' (Jn 13:52). Why should we not also enter this great stream of Joy?" (EG: 5)

That evening I returned to the sacristy and began to set up the image so it could be viewed and reverenced by any visitors who might arrive in the following days. My basic objective was to create a "sacred space" that would be equal to the reverent love the Mexican people have for Our Lady of Guadalupe. I found a big, heavy easel that was so perfect it seemed as if it had been custom made for displaying the cut-out image. Since the image was in an alcove, it was easy to section it off with kneelers and thus create a shrine effect. It was also possible to illuminate the alcove separately with a dim light which would help to create a more intimate, spiritual environment for prayer. Then I surrounded the image with flowers, candles, and two large angels that were stored in the sacristy. The angels were kneeling with their hands folded in prayer. I set up a little terracotta dish on a stand so we could burn a chip of incense periodically, and then… the finishing touch; Gregorian Chant playing softly in the background.

The next morning, Wednesday, Fr. Bob and I went over to the sacristy to make sure the shrine was ready to receive the faithful. As we approached the entrance to the sacristy we discovered 5 people from out of town who told us they had been there all night. They spent the night in prayer, waiting for the sacristy to be opened so they could reverence the image. When we entered the sacristy, all of us agreed that the little *capilla* (chapel) was perfect and provided a worthy context for the profound devotion that would, no doubt, be expressed there.

One of the things Fr. Bob and I discussed and believed to be of the highest priority was that this special moment should not go to waste but should, from a pastoral perspective, be taken advantage of. We decided to take turns hearing confessions as the pilgrims exited our homemade shrine. We set up a little confession station in a far corner of the sacristy and it worked out really well. I heard confessions from 9am to 12 noon… then Fr. Bob from 1pm to 3pm… then me from 3pm to 5pm… then Fr. Bob from 7pm to 10pm. The confessions were beautiful! After opening one's heart to the loving presence of La Virgencita, pouring out one's soul to Jesus in the sacrament of reconciliation was easy!

Around 12 noon, a big tour bus pulled into the Church parking lot. As the visitors exited the bus and strolled past the rectory we stepped outside to find out what was going on. "We're here to see the image", one woman said, "we came all the way from San

Antonio!" Fr. Bob and I looked at each other with a mixture of fear and astonishment. "You look surprised? Don't be… 2 more buses are on their way! And in an hour or so, a couple of buses should be arriving from Houston!" she added with glee. We politely excused ourselves and bolted back into the safety of the rectory realizing that the situation was now completely out of control!

"On Monday, this was a normal South Texas parish," I exclaimed, "now, only 2 days later, it's a National Shrine! Food vendors are starting to arrive… and what next? Someone will probably show up with a mobile gift shop to sell souvenirs and T-Shirts bearing an imprint of the image! Come tomorrow there could be buses arriving from other States… and the following day, maybe flights from other countries! By the time our superiors return, they won't even recognize the place!"

Fr. Bob and I were immersed in wonder and rejoiced in the Holy Spirit! We were so overwhelmed with joy because now it was absolutely clear that this was something God himself was doing; our part in it was irrelevant, and we probably couldn't have stopped it had we wanted to. Nevertheless, we felt like we were starring in a *Laurel and Hardy* movie where the 2 simpletons are left in charge of a store for a short period of time and somehow manage to turn the shop upside down!

By mid- afternoon, the area was flooded with pilgrims and media crews. I tried to work my way through the crowd as I headed over to the sacristy to hear confessions. I was trying to keep a low profile as I moved along but an eagle-eyed reporter spotted me. "We're live at St. Anthony's in Robstown, TX, covering the amazing story of the miraculous image of Our Lady of Guadalupe. We're speaking with one of the priests stationed here at the parish. Father, tell us… what are your thoughts regarding the image?" "It's very beautiful!" I responded. "Do you believe the image is supernatural?" pressed the reporter. "I believe the image is beautiful… only the

Bishop can speak to the actual nature of the image," was my reply. "But there must be something spiritual going on here," continued the reporter, "Can you tell us then... why have all these pilgrims come here?" "These people are here because they love their mother... it's as simple as that!" And with that, I excused myself and hurried into the sacristy.

"To understand this reality we need to approach it with the gaze of the Good Shepherd, who seeks not to judge but to love. Only from the affective connaturality born of love can we appreciate the theological life present in the piety of Christian peoples, especially among their poor." (*EG*, 125)

When I arrived at our homemade confessional, Fr. Bob took me aside. "Fr. Larry, you're not going to believe what's happening," he said... his speech much more animated than normal, "There have been numerous healings! One woman was carried into the chapel by her two sons. They placed her on a kneeler and she began to weep and pray. Then, all of a sudden, she stood up perfectly straight and walked out unassisted! Then there was a young woman who was on her way to have an abortion and a friend convinced her to stop and visit the image first. When she saw *La Virgencita* and the profound love and devotion of the humble pilgrims, she broke down in tears and decided right then and there to bring her baby to term and to raise the child as a loving mother."

Thursday was pretty much a repeat of Wednesday, except the crowd was bigger, the healings more numerous, and the presence of the media much more pervasive. We both realized that, although the spiritual momentum was growing steadily, it could stop on a dime... depending on the Bishop's decision regarding the actual nature of the image. We didn't waste much time thinking about that possibility, however, because it was so obvious that even if it all came to a screeching halt, it still would have been well worth it.

That evening we began to ponder our fate. What would be

the reaction of our superiors when they returned the following day, only to discover that the parish they had entrusted to us was now unrecognizable and was on its way to becoming a National Shrine? For some reason we felt that everything would be fine and they would not be upset with us. Our consciences were clear... we had been swept along by a spiritual joy that was so deep we were still under its tranquilizing influence.

Pastors spend a great deal of time and energy struggling with the question of how to renew their parish. Who would have guessed that all it takes is to put two inexperienced (but sincere!) priests in charge of the parish for a few days and the Lord will see their innocent unwillingness to interfere in his work as an invitation to renew the parish himself! OK... I'm just being facetious; but that does seem to be what happened in this particular case. Human beings can't plan this type of thing... only God can.

When our superiors returned Friday afternoon I was sitting in the rectory dining room reading the newspaper. Fr. Flanagan and Fr. Vince, the Pastor of St. Anthony's, entered the room. I continued to read the paper, wanting to appear calm... as though everything was normal and under control. "Hi, Fr. Larry," said Fr. Vince, sounding like he was in a good mood. "Oh, hi, Fr. Vince... Hello, Fr. Jim... welcome back." I responded... and then quickly turned my attention back to the newspaper, trying to look as nonchalant as possible. "Fr. Larry", said Fr. Vince, "why are there so many cars everywhere... and why are there tour buses parked in the Church parking lot?"

"Oh, those... I guess they're here to see the image," I replied in a matter-of-fact way... and immediately returned to the newspaper. "What image?" he shot back. I proceeded to give him the short version of the story, hoping to make it sound like it was something normal that happens in every parish. "You haven't seen the image yet?" I said. "No... where is it?" replied Fr. Vince. "It's in

the sacristy... just follow the line of people... you're going to love it!" Fr. Vince said nothing. "Watch out for the reporters!" I warned. With that Fr. Vince and Fr. Jim went out the back door of the rectory, and using whatever stealth they could muster, slipped into the sacristy to view the image of *La Virgencita*... along with her devoted children.

When the two superiors returned to the rectory I was still in the same chair with my head buried in the same newspaper. I looked up and watched them as they sat down at the dining room table. Something struck me immediately... they appeared visibly different compared to how they looked when they left the room 10 minutes before. Their faces were relaxed and seemed to radiate a mysterious peace. Clearly, they were moved by what they witnessed in *la capilla*. "Fr. Larry... does the Bishop know about the image?" Fr. Vince asked with a concerned look on his face. "I would imagine he does... the story has been covered by every newspaper and TV Station in Texas," I replied. "Have you had any communication with him about this?" questioned Fr. Vince. "No," I said. "Has the Bishop said anything yet regarding the nature of the image?" asked Fr. Vince. "No," I responded.

"If I did anything wrong here, I want to apologize," I said with sincerity, "we simply followed the joy we were experiencing in the depths of our souls... and we could see that the people were also experiencing this same mysterious joy! Our experience can be summed up in a line from one of the songs in *The Sound of Music*... 'How do you catch a cloud and pin it down!' We were helpless before the Joy of the Lord! Our only real option was to move with it. Did we do anything wrong?" "No!" said Fr. Flanagan, "No... not at all. You handled it well. The people are just wonderful... the love they are expressing for their mother is so beautiful! We'll wait and see what the Bishop says."

Fr. Vince asked me what was so interesting in the

newspaper. I told him I was reading a big article about the image: "Do you mind if I take a look?" he said. When he reached the part where the author of the article was describing *la capilla*, Fr. Vince lowered the paper, looked at me and said, "Fr. Larry... did you have to include Gregorian Chant in the background?" "Well..," I said, "I guess I got caught up in the moment... a bit over the top you think?" "Maybe... just a bit," he said with a big smile!

A couple of days later, the Bishop stated that although the image was lovely, and all the devotion expressed since its discovery praiseworthy, there was not sufficient cause to declare its origin to be supernatural. He did, however, allow the image to be placed in an alcove at the entrance of the Church so the faithful could continue to enjoy it and remember the wondrous parish renewal provided by the Lord himself!

"Expressions of popular piety have much to teach us; for those who are capable of reading them, they are a **locus theologicus** *which demands our attention, especially at a time when we are looking to the new evangelization."* (EG, 126)

Fr. Lawrence Edward Tucker, SOLT

Chapter Six

TRUSTING IN HIS MERCY

I remember going to Mass on Sunday when I was a teenager only to find on various occasions that the parish priest I was expecting to see on the altar was not there. Instead, there would be a priest I did not know who would describe himself as being a missionary. I didn't completely grasp what that meant, but one thing I knew for certain... I always enjoyed the beautiful mission stories they would tell! I never dreamed that one day I would be a missionary who traveled throughout the USA to share my own mission stories.

One particular summer I had a couple of mission appeals in New England and consequently had the opportunity to visit with family and friends in New York. One of my friends owned a chain of religious goods stores. She had accumulated at least 20 boxes of religious items for me to bring back to the missions. Two other friends who were sacristans in large parishes collected a great assortment of things their parishes no longer needed but would be extremely useful in a mission setting. By the time I was done loading this generous donation of religious goods into my generously donated suburban, I could barely see anything out of the rear view mirror!

The plan was to deliver all of these items to a mission in a little town named Jimenez located on the Mexican side of the Rio Grande. The Bishop of that Mexican diocese, whom I knew, had mentioned that if I ever had the opportunity to help this mission in any way he would really appreciate it. The mission was blessed with three dynamic missionary sisters who belonged to a Mexican community. Unfortunately, there was no priest available to serve in the mission so Mass was not offered there on a regular basis. That spring, I had the pleasure of visiting the mission and providing the little town with its first Sacred Triduum; Holy Thursday, Good Friday, Easter Vigil, and Easter Sunday.

The sister's knew that the entire town would show up so we rented the biggest hall in the town… and it still wasn't big enough! I don't think anyone realized (apart from the Bishop) how much potential there was in this little town for the development of a robust parish. Having witnessed this amazing turnout, and knowing the amount of pastoral ministry required to serve that many people, it was clear to me that Jimenez was the perfect destination for my cargo of religious goods.

The journey from the New York metropolitan area to the Texas border city of Laredo would take 4 days of driving. I had done it many times before and was so accustomed to the route I could practically do it "in my sleep". My only concern was the drug-war that was taking place at that time along the Texas-Mexico border. The Zetas, a new and extremely violent cartel, was moving in on the Gulf Cartel that had been dominant in the Texas border area for many years. The turf war that ensued took on epic proportions and was more reckless and gruesome than anyone could have ever imagined. The social chaos created was so great commentators began wondering whether Mexico had in fact become a "failed state".

I checked a particular website that monitors the location of the drug-war and alerts travelers to the "hot-spots" that should be avoided. It indicated that the danger zone was the Mexican border town of Matamoros, which is just across the river from Brownsville, TX. Considering that Matamoros was more than 300 miles down-river from where I was headed, I eliminated the drug-war as a concern and went on to resolve other issues that needed to be addressed. I had to get new tires for the truck, change the oil, install new windshield wipers, research motel locations and prices, sort and pack the religious articles then load the truck in such a way that the 25+ boxes would not shift during the course of the 2000-mile cross-country excursion.

Finally, all systems said go and I was ready for blast off. The most difficult part of the trip is getting out of the New York Metro area. Once New York is in the rearview mirror, it's clear sailing. Although the truck was filled to the brim and much heavier than normal, it performed beautifully. The trip unfolded without a hitch, and I arrived at *La Casita de San Francisco* in Laredo, TX, at around 8pm. *La Casita de San Francisco* is not a retreat center… it's a little, free standing, swimming pool cabaña in the back yard of a benefactor's home. It's about the size of a small mobile trailer. It has a bathroom with a shower, as well as a tiny kitchen area (sink, microwave, college fridge). Then, there is what I liked to call the "Great Room". This main living area of the casita is a sprawling, 8' X 8'.

The evening of my arrival in Laredo, exhausted from the tedium of 4 full days on the road, I was in bed and asleep by 10:30pm. The following morning I headed west, up-river, to Eagle Pass, TX. Directly across the river from Eagle Pass, TX, is the Mexican border town of Piedras Negras. Piedras Negras means "black stones"… which is symbolic for coal. The hills surrounding Piedras Negras produce a large amount of the coal used in Mexico. My plan was to cross into Piedras Negras, MX, and then head up-river on the Rivereña until I reached Jimenez.

The Rivereña is a very narrow and extremely dangerous road that runs parallel to the river. The road is typically so dangerous that Br. Michael and I renamed it. We called it… *La Jornada de Los Muertos* (The Journey of The Dead). But before taking on the challenge of the Rivereña, one must clear customs. Missionaries are always bringing things to their missions, and the review at customs can sometimes take hours. I was very surprised the Aduana (Customs) didn't stop me, considering how every available space in my truck had a box in it. I took this as a sign of God's providence and went about my merry way. After passing through the heart of Piedras Negras, I worked my way out of the city and headed west to the Rivereña.

When I finally emerged from the city and picked up the Rivereña, I was surprised to find that there was absolutely no traffic on this normally heavily travelled road. Generally, one has to contend with 18 wheelers, huge coal trucks, and big buses… all of them moving at high speed. To make matters worse, not only is the road narrow… there are no shoulders. If your vehicle, or the oncoming vehicle, drifts more than a foot in either direction, the result would almost certainly be a deadly crash.

As I drove along, I felt greatly relieved by the complete absence of any other vehicle. Usually, a driver can expect to have at least one near-death experience when using this infamous road. This was the first time I was actually enjoying the Rivereña. I popped in a John Michael Talbot CD and began singing and praising the Lord! Jimenez is about midway between Piedras Negras and Acuña. Acuña, like Piedras Negras, is a Mexican border city with a bridge that spans the river and connects with a US border city. Jimenez, on the other hand, is a small town with no bridge-connection to the USA. The ride from Piedras to Jimenez is around 20 minutes.

After about 10 minutes on the Riverena, a car came from the opposite direction and passed me. I gave the vehicle a blessing thinking they might need it if there were any trucks somewhere behind me. Shortly after this I arrived in Jimenez and, once again, was surprised by the absence of traffic or activity of any kind. On a normal day, Jimenez is a bustling little town with people walking along the road, children playing in the park, and teens riding their horses up and down the old cobblestone streets. On this particular day, there wasn't a single person visible anywhere. I chalked it all up to the probability that there was some special event taking place in Acuña… perhaps the Circus or some such thing.

When I reached the convent, the sisters formed a line stretching from my vehicle into the house, and, passing each box from one person to the next, we proceeded to unload all the religious goods. I noticed a man walking towards us on the sidewalk and thought perhaps he was going to help us. When he got close enough, I said, "Buenos Dias!" He did not reply and just continued on his way.

After all the boxes were safely stored in the convent, we went into the sister's beautiful little private chapel, and I prepared to celebrate Mass. Following Mass, I was treated to an extraordinary home-cooked meal and a very pleasant conversation dealing mostly with the challenging pastoral situation the sisters were faced with. Despite the fact that Jimenez did not have a resident priest, the sisters had formed the Catholic people into a strong community and were accomplishing great things with them. Should a priest become available to serve full-time in Jimenez, he would find it very easy to transform the mission into a viable parish.

Having said "Adios" to the sisters, I hopped into my truck and headed out of town to begin my return trip to Piedras. As I left Jimenez a pickup truck carrying two men pulled out of a side street and followed me onto the Rivereña. The pickup drove up close and began to tailgate me. I thought, "How silly… there are no cars anywhere on the road… why don't you just pass me!" Finally, after about half a mile of riding my bumper, the pickup passed me on the left and took off like a rocket! Within moments it was completely out of sight.

I reached the International Bridge at a bad time and was delayed an hour due to the heavy traffic. Eventually, after 4 hours on the road, I was back in Laredo, TX, enjoying the peace and tranquility of *La Casita de San Francisco*. The whole trip had been quite the one day marathon, and it wasn't long before I was sound asleep on my little bunk in the casita's "Great Room". I remembered that the only thing I had on my schedule for the following day was a dinner appointment with a family I knew. This being the case, I immediately decided to take a shot at *Rip Van Winkle's* record!

I hadn't seen Pablo for about a year and it was, as always, a real pleasure to see him and his beautiful family. Pablo, like many people in Laredo, was a licensed U.S. customs broker. But unlike many customs brokers in Laredo, Pablo owned and was the CEO of his own successful customhouse brokerage firm. Hardly anyone knows the border area as well as a customs broker, due to the fact that the broker's livelihood depends upon an accurate and up-to-the-minute knowledge of events that impact both sides of the border. As a missionary to northern Mexico, having a knowledgeable friend like Pablo was a tremendous blessing... his "intel" was always spot-on.

During the course of a very enjoyable dinner Pablo asked me why I was in Laredo. I told him about my 4-day journey from New York and how I had crossed into Piedras yesterday and taken the Riverena west to Jimenez where I met with the sisters and delivered the religious articles. Pablo turned white and dropped his fork, "Fr. Larry... let me check and see if I heard you correctly. You crossed into Piedras Negras, Mexico... *yesterday?*" "Yes", I responded. "Then you drove on the *Riverena* to Jimenez?" "Yes", I said.

"Fr. Larry", said Pablo... his voice trembling a bit, "Fr. Larry... you shouldn't even be sitting here in front of me! You should be dead and buried back there on the Riverena!" "Why, Pablo... I don't understand?" I replied, in a state of shock. "Fr. Larry", Pablo began, "didn't you get one of the flyers they were handing out all over Laredo the day before yesterday?" "No", I said, "I arrived late that evening and went right to sleep."

Pablo went on to explain that the purpose of the flyer was to warn people not to cross into Mexico the following day because *El Chapo*, the leader of the *Sinaloa Cartel*, had announced that on that day his "army" would come into the area and completely wipe out *Los Zetas*. El Chapo despised the Zetas for breaking the long standing, unwritten code observed by all the Mexican drug lords. According to this code, narco-traffickers agreed never to harm an innocent civilian or a member of law enforcement. They knew this kind of mayhem would put them in the spotlight and inevitably hurt their business. El Chapo, therefore, said he would come to the aid of the Mexican people and take out the Zetas; something the Mexican military had not yet been able to do. The Zetas responded with an announcement of their own saying that any vehicle that dared to use the Rivereña on that day would automatically be blown up (the Zetas felt certain that El Chapo's "soldiers" would be coming in on the Rivereña). The flyer added that this would end up being the bloodiest day in the history of Mexico!

I could hardly believe my ears! Not once did I feel as though I was in any kind of danger. "Fr. Larry", said Pablo, "could you tell me a little more about your trip... for example, what was the Rivereña like? I'll bet there was zero traffic!" "That's right Pablo, mine was the only vehicle on the... hold it... wait a second. Actually, there was one other vehicle... a car... it passed me coming from the opposite direction. I remember because I gave it a blessing." "Fr. Larry," said Pablo, "that car you blessed contained the Zeta scouts! They checked you out then reported back by cell phone to the men positioned along the Rivereña who were armed with bazookas and grenade launchers! You were directly in their crosshairs, Fr. Larry... and you didn't have a clue!"

"You're right, Pablo, I had absolutely no idea whatsoever," I said, "In fact... I was singing and was as happy as could be! But I don't understand... the website I checked said the drug-war was in the vicinity of Matamoros, MX?" "It was, Fr. Larry... about 3 weeks ago," answered Pablo, "When did you check the website?" It was then that I realized what had happened. I checked the website, then went on to prepare for the trip… which took me a little more than 2 weeks. Throw in the 4 days of travel and you're up to about 3 weeks. The war moved because of El Chapo's threat… and I was completely out-of-the-loop regarding this new development.

"Fr. Larry… what was Jimenez like when you arrived there?" Pablo questioned. "Very strange, Pablo… there wasn't a single person visible anywhere. Of course, I didn't think much of it at the time. Wait… now that I'm thinking of it… there was one person… a guy who looked to be around 30 years old. He passed us on the sidewalk as we were unloading the boxes. He had a rather mean looking countenance, but I greeted him anyway… and he didn't respond."

"Of course not, Fr. Larry," said Pablo, "he was another Zeta scout! They had 'eyes' on you, Fr. Larry! When you turned into Jimenez, and didn't continue on to Acuña, they wanted to see where you were going and what you were planning to do with all those mysterious boxes." Pablo continued, "So tell me, Fr. Larry, what was the return trip like? Can you remember anything strange that happened?"

"Yes", I said, "Two guys in a pickup pulled out of a side street and followed me on to the Rivereña. They rode my bumper and haunted me for about half a mile… then they passed me and took off at high speed until they disappeared over the horizon." "Zetas, Fr. Larry… they were Zetas," Pablo explained, "They were sending you a message… 'don't ever try this again, priest!'… that's basically what they were trying to tell you." "Well," I said, "I didn't get their message because I wasn't even aware I was doing something 'wrong'! At that moment, the Zetas and I were in two different worlds; they saw me as a bold intruder… and I saw them as nothing more than a pair of foolish ranchers!"

"Listen to me, Fr. Larry," said Pablo, "and you will see why what happened to you yesterday was nothing short of a miracle. Fr. Larry… you know how I make a living? With trucks… trucks that transport various products across the international border. My trucks use the Rivereña all the time. For the past 2 weeks, never mind yesterday… I couldn't get a single driver to use the Rivereña. The Zetas have been setting up road blocks and stealing vehicles… especially suburbans (they're perfect for transporting their 'warriors' to a battle). They usually beat and rob the passengers. Sometimes, they kidnap them or kill them on the spot if they resist in any way. They have claimed, and basically 'own' the Rivereña."

This is why, according to Pablo, the Zetas should have, at the very least, stopped me to see who I was and what I had in the boxes. Then, in order to protect their reputation for violence, they should have roughed me up, taken my truck, and made me walk back to Piedras Negras. By many accounts, the Zetas have taken on the cult of *La Santa Muerte* (The Holy Death)… which is condemned by the Catholic Church. And, just as they did with the practice of drug trafficking, reinventing it with a degree of violence unheard of in the past, the Zeta revision of La Santa Muerte was so fanatical it could be aptly described as the condemned version on steroids!

This being the case, one would not expect them to show any deference to a Catholic priest. But absolutely nothing happened to me. In fact, it was almost as if they escorted me to Jimenez! Were they, for some convoluted reason (and perhaps without even realizing it), protecting me from falling into the hands of El Chapo's men? We will never know. But based on everything Pablo shared, I had to agree that the entire affair seemed to have taken place on a different, higher plane.

I returned to the casita that evening in a state of awe and confusion: why did the Lord protect me to the degree that he did? I was mesmerized by the whole incident and pondered how I had been thoroughly immersed in mortal danger, yet had absolutely no awareness of it. As my friend pointed out... I was truly in the crosshairs! Why didn't they blow up my truck? Who decided that I should be spared? Why did they handle me with kid-gloves and not even question me? Why didn't the sisters say anything regarding the situation?

As I lay on my bed trying to fall asleep, these were the kind of questions that troubled me. I asked the Lord, in the prayerful solitude of *La Casita*, why I had not been harmed in any way. I felt as though he was saying, "because I was with you." I responded by saying, "Lord... as your servant, I know you are always with me. But this, Lord... this was just extraordinary! I mean... they didn't even pull me over!" Then... in the midst of the quiet, I sensed his reply. "On that day, I was... *REALLY* with you!"

It was then... and only then, that everything started to make sense. In the event the sisters might ask me to make some sick calls, on the morning I left for Jimenez I stopped into an Adoration Chapel to load my pix with consecrated hosts. And so, for the duration of my mission journey, Jesus... the Divine Son of the Eternal Father... was in my pocket! I couldn't have had more protection had I been surrounded by *Seal Team Six*! I reasoned that the eternal, unfathomable love of the Father for his Son was very much in play, and the Father's mercy was in fact *REALLY* present with me... "As the Father has loved me... so I have loved you" (Jn 15:9). An essential part of missionary life is simply trusting in our Father's mercy. Without this trust, we would probably feel paralyzed and unable to follow our Master as faithful missionary disciples.

"The Church's closeness to Jesus is part of a common journey; 'communion and mission are profoundly interconnected.' In fidelity to the example of the Master, it is vitally important for the Church today to go forth and preach the Gospel to all: to all places, on all occasions, without hesitation, reluctance or fear." (EG, 23)

Chapter Seven

LOVING AS JESUS LOVES

How do missionary communities acquire their missions? I used to wonder about this question… until I became a missionary and the secret was revealed to me. The short answer to this question is, in one sense, probably more mundane than most people would imagine. It's as simple as this… the phone rings! The call could come from any Bishop in the world needing missionary assistance in his diocese. The Bishop will usually explain how he learned about the missionary community then go on to describe to the best of his ability the particular need he has. If the community thinks they might be able to help the Bishop they will generally send someone to evaluate the mission.

Because of my familiarity with northern Mexico, I was asked to go on one of these fact-finding missions. The Bishop needed missionaries to take care of a rural mission parish in a small town hidden away in the mountains. I wasn't familiar with that particular town, but I did know some interesting facts about that area; the year round median temperature is 72°F, and the region is considered to have the most perfect climate in North America. Consequently, there is no need for heating or air-conditioning in the homes; which explains why a number of religious communities have set up their retirement facilities there. Also, because of the pristine beauty of the surrounding mountains, along with their evergreen forests, the area is affectionately known as *"La Suiza de Mexico"* (the Switzerland of Mexico).

I was told that the parish had a convent, a retreat center, and a number of outlying missions. Based on the initial description, it seemed like something our community could handle. Accepting pastoral responsibility for a mission, however, is not something any community treats lightly. Therefore, in order to be certain, the community administrators needed more information.

I was ecstatic at having been chosen for this assignment and wasted no time in contacting Brother Michael. This was certainly the kind of mission in which Brother Michael's phenomenal memory would be extremely helpful. There's really no substitute for team ministry… two heads are always better than one! Hopefully, between the two of us, we could gather sufficient info to facilitate a good decision regarding this potential mission. Brother was more than willing to accompany me, and began packing immediately.

My vehicle at the time was a 15-year-old, 4-Cylinder Nissan pickup truck with over 200,000, rough-and-tumble mission miles on it. Would the little truck make it from Corpus Christi, TX, to the mountains of northern Mexico? Of course, it would! That little white truck could make it from South Texas to *Tierra Del Fuego*, Chile… and back… without any problem! The Mexican people who were familiar with the truck called it… *La Camioneta Milagrosa* (the miracle pickup truck) because it appeared to be invulnerable and shielded from the negative developments associated with very old, high mileage vehicles. Once, while crossing the entire length of Florida on my way to a mission appeal in Miami, I drove directly through the heart of a raging Tropical Storm. What happened to La Camioneta Milagrosa? Absolutely nothing! In fact… I would say the truck's overall condition was improved because of the storm; I don't remember ever seeing the truck so clean and shiny!

After six hours on the road, we arrived and were immediately taken with the classic beauty of the little town. The parish Church was lovely and quaint, as were the quiet cobblestone streets and the tree-lined zocalo. Burro drawn carts and people on horseback were the finishing touch to this tranquil, bucolic scene. One of the great things about small town Mexico is that just about every street leads to the parish Church. This system works great if what you're looking for is in fact the parish Church. If, however, you're looking for a private home... good luck; most of the properties are not marked with numbers. In a small town where everyone knows everyone, house numbers are superfluous.

The pastor was most gracious and welcomed us with open arms. He immediately gave us a tour of the very large rectory, as well as the Church, convent, and retreat center. Based on what the pastor had shown us, it was clear that the facilities would be perfect for our community. It was now 2:00pm so we went to the rectory for *La Comida*, which is the main meal of the day. We told the pastor how impressed we were with the facilities and how appropriate they would be for our particular community. Then we asked him about the missions associated with the parish.

My face lit up when he told us there were over 40 mission stations! Most mission parishes have responsibility for no more than 10 mission chapels. Forty mission stations were the most I ever heard of, but I was excited because I knew our community would be able to do fantastic work with them. The pastor, however, must have misinterpreted my reaction because he immediately went into damage-control mode. "You must keep in mind, Fr. Larry, the vast majority of these missions are very small with no more than 30 or 40 people at mass. And the furthest station is only an hour away. Most of the missions are visited only once every 4 to 6 months. We try to visit each mission at least twice a year. That's the best we can do. On the big feast days, many people come in from the hills to the parish Church."

"Fr. Larry," said the pastor, "tomorrow is Sunday... would you like to celebrate mass in one of the outlying villages?" Wow! This is music to my ears, I thought, "Yes, Padre... of course! In fact...

that's exactly why we are here. We want to see as much of the mission as possible." "Bueno!" replied the pastor, "I'm going to send you to one of the biggest mission chapels. I'll tell you how to get there in the morning. Please excuse me... I have some important business to take care of. I'll catch up with you at breakfast."

The following morning after breakfast Br. Michael and I were on our way to a little village tucked away in the evergreen forest. It was very easy to find, and when we arrived it was evident that the pastor did indeed send us to one of the largest mission stations. We saw many people coming to the chapel from every direction. When I entered the little Church, the female sacristan was there to greet me. "Bienvenidos, Padre!" she said, "Thank you for coming to celebrate mass for us."

After greeting the sacristan, I asked her if everything was ready to begin mass. "All the people are here," she said, "but the altar is not ready. Did you bring the mass kit?" "Mass kit? *What* mass kit? No one said anything about a mass kit!" I thought to myself. The sacristan said the chapel did not have any of the items necessary for mass. Normally, she said, the priest brought everything with him. "The pastor forgot to tell me about the need for a mass kit," I said in my defense, "and, since he said it was one of the largest chapels, I guess I just assumed everything would be here." The sacristan stared at me with a puzzled look on her face, as if at any moment I was going to say, "Hey, lighten-up... I'm just kidding!"

"Padre", said the sacristan, "what are we going to do?" I looked towards the altar and noticed there was a lit sanctuary lamp. "Are there consecrated hosts in the tabernacle?" I asked. "Si, Padre... there are," She responded. "OK, then... I guess we will just have to shift gears and have a communion service," I said... feeling terrible, but thinking the problem was solved. "No, Padre... you don't seem to understand. These people haven't had Mass in four months! They know the difference between a communion service and Mass. They

are here for Mass, Padre. Many of them have walked for hours to get here. Everyone will be greatly disappointed if you don't celebrate a Mass."

"I understand," I said, "Let's see what we can do." I walked down the center aisle, went into the sanctuary, and stood in front of the altar facing the congregation. As I looked out at these beautiful, humble people… most of whom seemed to be indigenous, I was unable to articulate a single word. Their deep desire for Mass was clearly visible in their reverent demeanor. How could I deliver such a disappointing message? Somehow, I summoned the strength to explain the situation to them. Some seemed confused… but most looked devastated! Up until this point I was still considering the possibility of a communion service. But after seeing for myself how devout the people were, a communion service was completely out of the question. It was time for plan "B".

"I know how much Mass means to you," I said, "so we are going to try something." I glanced over at Br. Michael who was sitting off to the side with a bewildered look on his face. "Does anyone here have a nice cup that we could use as a chalice?" "Yes, Father, I have one. I will go get it!" offered a generous parishioner. "Bueno… does anyone have a little plate that could serve as a paten?" "Si, Padre… I'll be right back with it!" said an enthusiastic young man. "Good… we're getting there," I said. At the same time though, I have to admit… with all the unusual questions and answers, I was starting to feel like a game show host! "Does anyone have a little wine we can put in our new chalice?" "Yes, Father, I have a bit… and I believe it's still good!" "Thank you," I said, "this is great… we're just about there. Br. Michael has the monthly missal, and I have some old vestments in the truck. Now all we need is one unconsecrated host."

I turned to the sacristan, who was standing nearby, and asked her if there were any hosts in the sacristy. "No, Padre. The priests don't use the sacristy. They never even go in there," she said, "They go directly to the altar and set up. Then they celebrate the Mass, process out, and leave." "So there are no hosts in the sacristy... not even one?" I questioned. "Si, Padre... not a single one. You see, Father... sometimes we go for six months without a Mass, so the priests have learned from experience not to leave anything perishable here," she replied, with sadness in her voice.

At this point, things were not looking good. We had come a long way, only to run into a roadblock right before the finish line. I could think of no solution to this dilemma. The flow of ideas had completely dried up. I tried my best, but it wasn't good enough. Then, owning my inescapable littleness, and not fully comprehending what I was doing, I turned to the congregation and said, "See that tabernacle? Jesus is there!" With this statement, I could tell the people thought I was about to announce a communion service. "And since Jesus is here with us... we are all going to kneel and silently beg him to give us an unconsecrated host."

What was I doing? What if this didn't work? Even though I asked myself these questions, I was under the inspiration of the Spirit and there was no turning back. I knelt down in front of the altar with my back to the people, closed my eyes and began to pray. The Church was blanketed with such a profound silence, not even the normal sounds of people breathing could be heard. A blind person would have thought it was an empty Church, but I can assure you, that little Church was packed!

"A true missionary, who never ceases to be a disciple, knows that Jesus walks with him, speaks to him, breathes with him, works with him. He senses Jesus alive with him in the midst of the missionary enterprise." (EG, 266)

I started to consider the possibility that the people were probably giving up on me. I pictured them sneaking out the main entrance of the chapel... one by one. I turned around very slowly to see if this was the case and was truly moved by what I saw. The first few pews were filled with children and all of them had their eyes closed, their hands folded for prayer, and their heads humbly tilted forward. That was all I needed to see. If the little children were that rapt in prayer, I knew from experience that everyone else was equally focused.

"Lord", I said, within myself, "look at your beautiful people! Look at how humble and sincere they are. Look how they have turned to you, trusting in your mercy and love. And what are they asking for? Not a better house… not food, clothes, or medicine… all of which they desperately need. No, Lord… they are asking for you! This is not hard for you, Lord… you can do this. You hear the cry of the poor, Lord … please, give us one unconsecrated host!"

The sacristan, who was kneeling about 5 feet away from me, quietly shuffled over to my side and whispered in my ear, "Padre… how is the Lord going to give us an unconsecrated host?" As if I wasn't befuddled enough… now I have the sacristan asking me the question of the day! I guess the mere fact that I proposed such an audacious solution in the first place made me look like *The Amazing Kreskin.* In any case, I couldn't help but be deeply moved by her faith and innocence. Notice… she didn't ask *if* the Lord would send a host, but *how* would he send it. As a dutiful sacristan, she was really asking if she should be getting something ready for the arrival of the host.

"I don't know how the Lord will give us a host," I whispered to her, "but don't worry… it's his problem… he will figure it out." The sacristan seemed to be more or less satisfied with this answer, although she still appeared a bit uneasy. It's strange, but the question of how the Lord would provide a host never even entered my mind. During this whole time, I never gave it a single thought. The Spirit must have taken over because I simply knew the

Lord could and would do it. My job was not to know everything… my job was to *ask* for everything!

As I knelt there in silent prayer, a scene from scripture gently passed through my mind. It was Mt 17: 24-27… the story of how Jesus was asked to pay the temple tax. In response, Jesus sent Peter to a nearby pond telling him to cast in a line and he would catch a fish. The fish, Jesus said, would have a coin in its mouth, and that coin would be the exact amount needed to pay the tax. This scriptural episode unfolded within me and I thought nothing of it. In fact, it made me feel like I wasn't really praying but instead was beginning to fall asleep.

"What an unworthy priest I am," I thought to myself, "Here I am, daydreaming about colorful scripture passages and I'm supposed to be praying for a host! I have to pull myself together and focus." But then I thought, "Hey, hold on, I am praying. In fact, it was my idea to pray for a host. There must be something in that scripture scene… something that pertains to our situation." I ran the whole scene through my mind once more… slowly.

Suddenly, it hit me! I don't really understand it, but somehow I knew what the Spirit was trying to tell me. Without getting up from my kneeling position, I signaled the sacristan to come over to me. "Señora," I whispered, "are there any books in the sacristy?" "No," she responded, "wait… yes," she said, "There's one old, dusty book." "Good," I said, "I need you to go into the sacristy, pick up that old book, turn it upside down, and leaf through the pages like this (using my hands, I demonstrated how to do it)."

The sacristan knelt there and stared at me as though she was looking at a priest who had just provided her with irrefutable evidence that he was completely insane! It was easy to read her mind… her thoughts were written all over her face. "Why did they send us this *loco* gringo priest? First… he forgets the mass kit. Then, he has everyone praying for a host. Now, he's asking me to go into the sacristy and play around with an old book... as if I were a *bruja* (witch) or something!"

"Father, why would I do that? It doesn't make any sense!" she protested gently in a low whisper. "Señora, please... trust me. This is our only chance." I pleaded with her... looking into her eyes and trying to appear as rational as possible (all things considered!). "OK," she said, "I will do it." And with that she rose carefully from her kneeling position then, slowly and very deliberately, walked over to the sacristy. I could tell by the dour expression on her face she was thinking this ridiculous experiment was just moments away from its disastrous conclusion.

The sacristan was in the sacristy for no more than a minute when we heard her cry out at the top of her lungs... "UN MILAGRO! ES UN MILAGRO! (A miracle! It's a miracle!). A HOST CAME OUT OF THE BOOK!" She emerged from the sacristy holding up a host in her right hand for everyone to see!

The whole congregation jumped to their feet and went into "overdrive" with *gritos* (happy shouts), applause, and songs of praise... "Demos gracias al señor... demos gracias... demos gracias al señor!" (We give thanks to the Lord!). The people were so happy and so very grateful that God had responded to their prayer, they almost forgot where they were and why they were there!

"I can say that the most beautiful and natural expressions of joy which I have seen in my life were in poor people who had little to hold on to." (EG, 7)

I took the host, placed it on the paten, then vested and began the mass... "en el nombre del Padre, y del Hijo, y del Espíritu Santo!" Of course, there was no need for an entrance procession or an opening song... the people were still in a state of wild jubilation! And what a mass it was! Everyone was spiritually elevated and rejoiced because the Lord had responded to their heartfelt desire to be one with him in his paschal mystery.

During this wondrous mass of thanksgiving, I couldn't help but reflect on the marvels I had witnessed in that remote, little chapel. I thought about how the Mexican government might not even know these people exist... let alone care about them. Their heavenly Father, on the other hand, truly cared for them and knew each one by name. And, like any good father, he was determined to feed his beloved children, whatever it took. If he had to find a priest in New York and send him to a distant mountain hideaway in Mexico... he would do it. If he had to compensate for the natural limitations of his servant by taking charge of the situation himself... he would. That's how profound his love is for people the world usually looks upon as totally insignificant. They are *his* children and *he* will feed them!

When mass was finished, I processed down the center aisle and out the entrance of the chapel to the sidewalk. Out of the corner of my eye, I spotted a dark pickup truck speeding down the dirt road that leads to the chapel. The truck drove right up to the chapel, and, in a cloud of dust, skid to a stop. A young man, who was clearly very excited, leaped out of the truck... "Padre Lorenzo! Padre Lorenzo! My name is Raul... I'm a seminarian. I have the mass kit, Padre! I brought you the mass kit!"

"Gracias, Raul, thank you... how very kind of you. But we don't need it. You see, Raul... we have faith. And with a Father as loving as ours, that's all we really need!"

"The Church, guided by the Gospel of mercy and by love for mankind, hears the cry for justice and intends to respond to it with all her might.' In this context we can understand Jesus' command to his disciples: 'You yourselves give them something to eat!' (Mk 6:37): it means working to eliminate the structural causes of poverty and to promote the integral development of the poor, as well as small daily acts of solidarity in meeting the real needs which we encounter." (EG, 188)

IMAGES OF JOY

FATHER JAMES H. FLANAGAN

Founder

Society of Our Lady of the Most Holy Trinity

Born:
Ascension Thursday, May 29, 1924

Baptized:
Trinity Sunday, June 15, 1924

Ordained to the Sacred Priesthood:
January 10, 1952

Founded the Society of Our Lady
of the Most Holy Trinity:
July 16, 1958

Entered Eternal Life:
Holy Thursday, March 24, 2016

 SOCIETY OF OUR LADY
OF THE MOST HOLY TRINITY
www.solt.net

Front Photo by John Spink
©2016 Society of Our Lady of the Most Holy Trinity

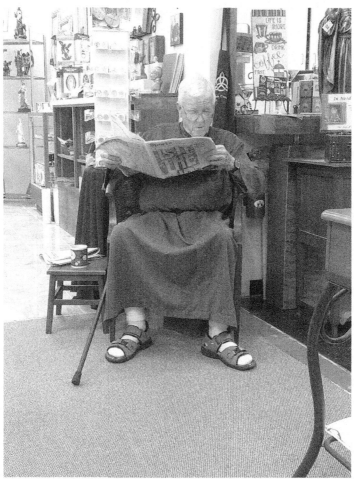

Fr. John McHugh, age 91 in 2014

Seminarian Larry on horseback in Guatemala (1988)

SOLT volunteer, Alan Howard, taking snapshots in a Mayan village in Guatemala (1988)

Fr. John M. in front of a mission chapel in Guatemala (1988)

Children playing next to the church in Benque Viejo, Belize (1988)

Fr. John McHugh and a SOLT sister in the Peten
on their way to a Mayan village (1988)

Seminarian Larry in Benque Viejo, Belize (1988)

Our Lady of Mt. Carmel Mission Church, Benque Viejo, Belize.
Seminarian Larry with his cousins, Rob and Erin. (1988)

Mayan Ruin, Xunantunich (1988)

Seminarian Larry on horseback in Guatemala (1988)

The rainforest of Benque Viejo, Belize (1988)

Fr. Larry, a SOLT volunteer,
and a SOLT lay member named Susie Zook
in Las Nuevas Colonias, Nuevo Laredo, MX (1998)

Fr. Larry in Nuevo Laredo, MX (1998)

Fr. Larry with a SOLT volunteer and a SOLT seminarian in Las Nuevas
Colonias, Nuevo Laredo, MX (1998)

Fr. Larry and Br. Michael in their last mission
in a little city in Northern Mexico named Muzquiz (2004)

Fr. Lawrence Edward Tucker, SOLT

ABOUT THE AUTHOR

Fr. Tucker was born on May 26th, 1955, in Manhattan, New York City. He is a bilingual missionary priest in *The Society of Our Lady of the Most Holy Trinity* and has served in Mexico, Belize, Guatemala, England, Texas, and New York.

Fr. Tucker holds an A.A. in Liberal Arts from Nassau Community College, Garden City, NY; a B.A. from St. Joseph's College, Patchogue, NY; and a Master of Divinity, as well as an M.A. in Theology from Holy Apostles Seminary, Cromwell, CT.

Fr. Lawrence Edward Tucker, SOLT

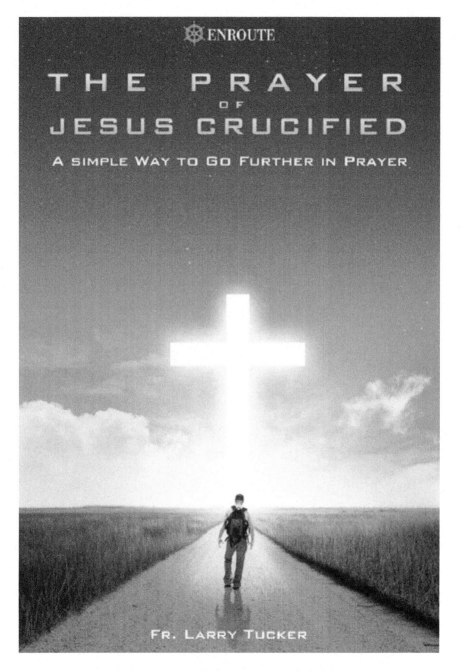

See also *The Prayer of Jesus Crucified* in both English and Spanish editions at http://enroutebooksandmedia.com/pojc/

Made in the USA
Middletown, DE
01 February 2022